GENESEE VALLEY PEOPLE
1743–1962

by Irene A. Beale

Chestnut Hill Press
Geneseo, New York

© 1983 by Irene A. Beale
All rights reserved. For information address Chestnut Hill Press, 5320 Groveland Road, Geneseo, N. Y. 14454
Library of Congress Catalog Card Number: 83-71772
ISBN: 0-9608132-1-7
Printed in the United States of America

To Jane and Martha

By the same author

William P. Letchworth: A Man for Others

Cover illustration from 1978 pencil drawing, "Genesee River Bend," by Paul H. Hepler

CONTENTS

Preface

What reason could I have had to bring these character sketches of fifty-some people together in one book? Apart from the fact that each of them had a certain distinction, they seem to have no more in common than their residence in the Genesee Valley. Nor did all of them express (as far as we know) special appreciation of its beauty, though some did so in words and others indirectly by their actions. Considered as an entity, they provide an introduction to the social history of nineteenth-century New York State, but that was not my purpose.

It was something else, a something I cannot adequately define. My delight in, and respect for, the miracle of personality is part of it. Even when we know so little about some of these people that it is like seeing them through the wrong end of a telescope, I feel a kinship with their joys and sorrows, their fears and hopes.

I understand, too, how Benedict Brooks (brother of Micah) felt. *The History of Wyoming County* states that sometime around 1840 Benedict, after sitting a long time in a musing mood, finally said, "Ansel Warren split and drew the rails and laid up half a mile of fence for me in a month, and I think I ought to have acknowledged my obligations to him more distinctly than I did."

These emotions make me want to share my enthusiasm with a wider audience than serious students of local history. I want to introduce my nineteenth-century friends to new readers so that, though they have died, in a sense they will still live.

I am indebted to Wendy Innis for skillfully editing my manuscript and grateful for the resources of the Genesee Valley Collection of the State University of New York at Geneseo's Milne Library and the University of Rochester Department of Rare Books, for study facilities at Milne Library and for the unfailing help of librarians of these institutions.

Mary Jemison's Later Life
and Her Descendants

When Dr. James Seaver wrote his biography of Mary Jemison (1743–1833) in 1823, he made her life-story up to the age of eighty known to many. Her later activities and information about her descendants, found only in scattered accounts, have been less well known.

A brief sketch of "the White Woman's" early life begins with the day in 1758 when Indians raided the Jemison home near Gettysburg, Pennsylvania, killing all the family except two brothers who escaped and fifteen-year-old Mary. She was taken on a forced march to what is now Pittsburgh and given to two Seneca women, who adopted her to take the place of a dead brother. Married to a Delaware, she had a son. When the baby was nine months old, her husband took her to visit relatives in the Genesee Valley.

Carrying her baby on her back and walking most of the way, this slight young woman reached Little Beard's Town, later Cuyler-ville, a distance of more than 600 miles. There she learned that her husband, who had dropped out of the trek, had died. She later married the Seneca Chief, Hiokatoo, and had six more children. Adapting to the role of a Seneca woman, Mary grew crops, tended stock, carried water, ground cornmeal, cared for children and cooked. The valley flatlands were so fertile that grass grew there high enough to hide a man on horseback. The river provided fish and the woods game.

Then in 1779 Sullivan's raid swept up from Newtown (now Elmira) to the Genesee Valley. The army destroyed forty Indian villages and 160,000 bushels of corn. Little Beard's Town was burned to the ground, Mary Jemison reporting that not enough

1

food was left to keep one child alive one day. The few survivors left for British-held Fort Niagara—all but Mary, who chose to stay in the Valley.

With her two youngest children on her back and the others tagging along, she walked to what later was called Gardeau Flats near Castile. There she hired out to two escaped Negro slaves, receiving some corn in payment for husking their crop. Over the next fifty-two years, she built a house, acquired livestock and eventually had tenants working the land on shares. When the Indians signed the treaty of the Big Tree in 1797, they lost all their Genesee Valley land except some small reservations and a tract of 18,000 acres which they gave to Mary. After that, trouble was piled on trouble: Hiokatoo died; then her son John killed his half-brother, his brother and later was himself killed. In 1823 Jemison sold all her land except two square miles for a pittance to Micah Brooks and Jellis Clute.

From having been one of but three or four white persons in the region, she became one of the few following Indian customs. She wore native dress, went barefoot in summer, slept on a bed of skins and ate sitting on the floor. Occasionally she visited some settlers in Canaseraga and once planned to stay with them overnight until Indians, not wanting her to be with whites more than several hours, came after her. Myron H. Mills, son of the founder of Mt. Morris, recalled that, except for her white skin, sandy hair and blue eyes, she resembled an Indian. "She was a peacemaker," he said, "and kept strictly to her own affairs." Henry O'Reilly, Micah Brooks's son-in-law, visited her, finding her at first reserved, but more talkative when she learned that he came from Ireland as she had.

"The White Woman" was known for her kindness and hospitality to both Indians and whites. As one acquaintance reported, "A person never need go from her door hungry, not even the beasts of the field." A settler in Orangeville whose crops had failed and who came to the Valley to buy corn told how she filled his sack with corn, refusing payment, and gave him supper. For the rest of his life, he claimed that Mary Jemison was the best cook he had ever known.

According to one story, a white man with a very dark complexion bought a tract of land next to hers. Seeing her coming toward him one day, he said to some companions, "Here comes

Mary Jemison. I'll have some fun with her." Then he asked her, "Mrs. Jemison, are you willing to join hands with me so that we own your land and mine in joint account? We can make it pay better to farm these lands together than separately."

Mary replied, "No, I have been married twice and each time to an Indian, and if I ever do marry again, I will marry a white man!"

Mary Jemison finally became tired of being considered an oddity in the white-dominated region and missed the company of her "own" people. She joined the Senecas on the Buffalo Creek Reservation on the outskirts of Buffalo. At the end of her life in 1833, she sent for a Christian missionary on the reservation. Greatly disturbed, she told her that she had forgotten the prayer her mother had taught her years ago. The missionary helped this little Irish-American-Indian lady to say the Lord's Prayer, bringing to a close the circle of her life.

Mary told Dr. Seaver in 1823 that she had thirty-nine grandchildren and fourteen great-grandchildren. She must have had mixed feelings about her own children: Thomas, son of her first husband, and the children of Hiokatoo, John, Jesse, Jane, Nancy, Betsy and Polly. Her three sons' lives ended violently, each death resulting from drunkenness. John had a curious combination of constructive and destructive tendencies. Mary described him as a doctor, saying that he was "considerably celebrated among the Indians of various tribes for his skill in curing diseases by the administration of roots and herbs." Yet this man killed his halfbrother, Thomas, and a year later his brother, Jesse. Five years afterward he himself was killed in a drunken brawl.

Fortunately, Mary's daughters were more comfort to her, although Jane died at around age fifteen. Of Betsy we know only that she married John Greenblanket, lived near her mother and had seven children. Nancy, the oldest, married Billy Greenblanket and also had seven children. It was for her that Mary built the house which William P. Letchworth later moved to its place beside the Indian Council House on his estate, now Letchworth State Park. An early settler of Portage recalled that Nancy owned many acres of wild plum trees, among which roamed her eighty horses. They ate the tree branches as high as they could reach, leaving a beautiful canopy of leaves overhead. Polly married George Shongo and had eight children.

Polly's son David, also called "Seneca" Shongo, went with his mother and grandmother when they left the Valley for the Buffalo Creek Reservation in 1831. One who knew him in the 1870's described him as childlike, affectionate and gentle. "With his long romantic locks of coal-black hair," this man wrote in a newspaper article, "his clear olive complexion, his large, melancholy eyes gazing at you from under the shadow of a slouched and plumed hat, his apparel clean yet thriftily patched, he looked . . . like a gypsy poacher or a Spanish contrabandero . . . "

This writer continued, "One theme is forever present in his thoughts. It is 'Genesee Valley—beautiful, beautiful country—far, far off. When we broke up and came away Grandmother sent me to gather the herds. I found most of them, but some had wandered away into the woods, and they no hear my call. We left some behind. I think they are there now looking for us. Often, often, I listen in the night, when it is still, and I hear them calling after me, 'Moo! Moo! Moo!' "

David's brother, James, also made the trek to Buffalo Creek. Said to have been his grandmother's favorite among Polly's children, he was then a boy of eleven and helped his mother and grandmother as much as he could. He was called "Dr. Shongo," as he was a healer, and he took part in Letchworth's "Last Council" of the Senecas and Mohawks, later helping him move Mary Jemison's remains for re-burial on Letchworth's Council Hill. He was described as "an intelligent and thoughtful man who enjoys the confidence and respect of his neighbors, white and red, to an enviable degree."

There is a great contrast in the lives of two children of Thomas, Mary's son by her first husband, Chief Sheninjee. One, James Jemison, lived near Portage with his wife, daughter and a medicine man called Dr. Silverheels. Suspicious of Silverheels's relationship with his daughter, James fought and killed him. He was sentenced to from three to five years in jail, and, though Letchworth and the trial judge were among those who petitioned to have the sentence revoked, he went to Auburn State Prison. Some time later he wrote to Letchworth:

> I want to tell you about myself. This is the first time I have gone to school. I could never write my name before. I learn quite good now. I read all kinds of books. I read geography; I comprend what is going on in this world. I read the Bible. I comprend the word of God. I can speak English language all right.

Very different was the fate of his brother, Thomas, who was named for their father. Buffalo Tom, as he was called, built a home on Squakie Hill in what is now Mt. Morris. He grew corn on the river flats and raised cattle which he sold to General William Mills. Later he ran a tavern on the Buffalo Creek Reservation, then operated a large farm on the Cattaraugus Reservation where he became quite prosperous. With his cousin, Dr. James Shongo, he took part in the Last Council. He was also a member of a delegation to President Andrew Jackson seeking his help in a land dispute and was given a solid silver medal. Three inches in diameter, it bore Jackson's likeness on one side and two crossed pipes—emblems of friendship—on the other. His son attended Dartmouth College, studied medicine in Buffalo and became an assistant surgeon in the United States Navy.

Handsome and more than six feet tall, Buffalo Tom was a commanding figure even in old age. He regretted that as a child he had spent only a few days at the school on Squakie Hill which he could have attended, but he spoke well and found others to write down his words. It was said of him that "being endowed by nature with more than ordinary intellectual powers, he learned much from observation and experience, and for half a century became a leading councilman and representative Indian in his tribe."

There seems to be only one exception to Buffalo Tom's success story. By his own admission, he was never good at hunting. His uncles, cousins and even his nephews tried to make a hunter of him. But he said, "They could not succeed. Deer always sees me first!"

SOURCES

Abrams, George H., Letter to author
Letchworth, William P., William P. Letchworth Papers
Seaver, James, *A Narrative of the Life of Mary Jemison*

Three Judicial Hosmers

Three of the many Hosmers of nineteenth-century Avon—a father, son and grandson—present three contrasting adaptations to the legal profession.

The first, Dr. Timothy Hosmer (c. 1745–1815), was, so to speak, drafted into the law. When the first judge of the Ontario County Court resigned, Hosmer was appointed to fill the vacancy. In this capacity he presided in the first case tried before a jury in an Ontario County Court of Record and served to the age of sixty. The historian, Lockwood R. Doty, himself a judge, termed him a capable one.

Yet Timothy Hosmer was foremost a physician. During the Revolution he had earned renown as an army surgeon. This was largely due to his having treated smallpox cases by vaccination, a discovery which Edward Jenner had recently advanced but which was not yet generally accepted. According to the historian, Orsamus Turner, he "espoused the new discovery with professional boldness and used it with great success." When Maj. John André was executed as a British spy, Hosmer was the medical officer who reported him dead. His diploma of membership in the Society of the Cincinnati, a fraternity of retired Continental Army officers, was signed by George Washington.

Coming to the Valley from Farmington, Connecticut, in 1790, Hosmer and a companion bought the land that is now Avon for themselves and three others, paying eighteen cents per acre. He settled there a year later and built a log house, the first residence of a white man in the area. In about 1800 he read Episcopal Church services in the settlement's log schoolhouse. It was he who named the community Hartford, which it was called until 1808.

As the only physician west of Canandaigua, Timothy Hosmer tended many patients and, as Turner recorded, was remembered in

6

many settlements for "his disregard of fatigue, his long night woods rides . . . , his good humor and the kind words he always had to cheer the desponding settler . . ." He was a good friend of the Indians, who showed their appreciation by naming him At-ta-gus, meaning "the healer of diseases." This healer may have learned from them, for one pioneer recalled his recommending butternut root as a cathartic.

Dr. Hosmer's library included classical literature, and his letters to his friends, James and William Wadsworth and Charles Williamson, reveal him as a poet and scholar. One writer noted that "his manner was courtly, and his dress corresponded," to which another added mention of his courtesy, saying that "when passing a lady acquaintance on the street, he would bow with head uncovered, though rain were falling." Certainly a distinguished man, he was, first, a physician, and, second, a judge.

His son, George, (1781–1861) in contrast, was a lawyer to his fingertips. When he began practice in Canandaigua in 1802, his first case was tried with his father presiding. A story is told of this event which characterizes both father and son. The lawyer opposing George Hosmer objected to some evidence he had introduced, and George defended himself. The Judge interrupted him, saying severely, "George, you are wrong."

"I think not. I believe I understand myself and I wish you to look at the point in this light," the young man answered, proceeding to explain his case.

"That won't do, George," said the Judge, again interrupting. "You don't comprehend the question at all."

"I think that is precisely the trouble with the Court," came the son's retort.

"Sit down, Sir!" thundered the father. George sat down, but was on his feet the next minute. "What do you mean, sir? Do you Think you can trifle with this Court?" roared the now-furious Judge.

"No, sir, I do not intend that, but I am determined to try this case and make you understand that I am George Hosmer, Esquire, Attorney and Counsellor at Law, and that you are nothing but a judge!"

For a long moment Timothy Hosmer looked down at his son, so astonished he could not speak. Finally recovering himself, he said, "Go on, sir. You have two excellent qualities for a lawyer. You have all the impudence of your forefathers and brass enough to carry it out." George then made his point, uninterrupted.

This lawyer began practice in Avon in 1808 with time out to serve as a major in the War of 1812. An incident which occurred during his years of private practice provides a balance to his confrontation with his father. In a situation in which the plaintiff's case depended upon a note, his lawyer had presented his case to the jury when he discovered he had left the note in his office. He was forced to tell Hosmer, the defendant's attorney, that he would have to submit to a non-suit. Hosmer immediately replied, "I scorn to take advantage of my friend under such circumstances. Let a juror be withdrawn and the panel discharged."

When Livingston County was organized in 1821, Hosmer became its first district attorney. He served in the State Assembly one year, gaining a reputation as a billiant orator, then was again district attorney for twelve years. The acknowledged leader of the Livingston County bar, he was associated with all the important trials of his time in Upstate New York. Obviously, a born lawyer.

Not so his son William Howe Cuyler Hosmer, (1814–1877) who could be called a reluctant lawyer, for his true love was poetry. After graduating from Temple Hill Academy in Geneseo and Geneva (now Hobart) College, he practiced law in Avon, then worked in the New York City Customs House. Though rejected from the Army during the Civil War, he, nevertheless, went with a New York Volunteers Battery to New Orleans and took part in an expedition with them. At this time one of his sons drowned; his other son was killed in battle and the next year his wife died. He, himself, came back to Avon in poor health.

But he did have the consolation of his writing. His mother had spoken several Indian languages, and her sympathy for the Indians had inspired William to study their culture, not only in Western New York, but also on trips to Wisconsin and Florida.

His best-known work is a long narrative poem, *Yonnondio, or Warriors of the Genesee: a Tale of the Seventeenth Century.* (The word, yonnondio, means "lament for the aborigines.") He had learned this and other legends from Horatio Jones, who, captured by Indians as a youth, later became an interpreter for them. Hosmer said he wrote this poem "to throw the mantle of romance over the pleasantest scenes of my boyhood." Many of his shorter poems show the poet's deep love of the Valley, as in "The

Markham Elm" in praise of a tree in Avon which was forty feet in circumference and shadowed an acre of ground. It begins,

> Like an old warrior with his helm
>   Decked grandly with a crest of green
> A thousand years has stood yon elm,
>   Chief glory of the scene.

Another example is:

> Mona-Sha-Sha
> A Legend of the Upper Falls
>
> Go, tourist, where the Genesee
> Takes rise among the southern hills,
> And, swollen by a thousand rills,
> Flows on at last unclogged and free!
>
> Go, tourist, where the Genesee
> In falling, shakes the solid land!
> Cam, Avon, Teviot and Dee
> Flow not through scenes more truly grand.

William H. C. Hosmer is seldom recalled as a lawyer. He must have preferred his title of "the Bard of Avon."

SOURCES

Doty, Lockwood L., *A History of Livingston County*
Doty, Lockwood R., *History of Livingston County*
"Hosmer, William Howe Cuyler," *Dictionary of American Biography*
Hosmer, W. H. C., *Lays and Lyrics*
_____, *The Poetical Works of W. H. C. Hosmer*
Livingston County Historical Society, *Annual Report, 1897*
Smith, James, *History of Livingston County, New York 1687-1881*
Turner, Orsamus, *History of the Pioneer Settlement of Phelps and Gorham's Purchase*

Nathaniel Rochester and a City Capable of Great Things

At age fifty-eight in 1810, Nathaniel Rochester (1752–1831) deserved a rest. He had served the Republic well both during and after the Revolution and worked hard to succeed in business. Moreover, he had not fully recovered from a violent illness contracted while on Army duty. He could have eased into the pleasant life of a retired southern gentleman. Instead, he founded and developed Rochester.

Nor was his move to New York State the first time he had begun a new career. In 1781 he had left a life as a merchant in North Carolina for Hagerstown, Maryland, where he operated both a nail and rope factory and a flour mill. In short order he was made a member of the State Legislature, a county court judge, county sheriff, presidential elector in the year of Madison's election and president of the Hagerstown bank.

The start of the new century was the year of Colonel Rochester's first visit to the Genesee Valley. Together with Maj. Charles Carroll and Col. William Fitzhugh, he rode on horseback to Bath and thence along the Williamson Road to Williamsburg, New York, to meet the land agent, Capt. Charles Williamson. On his advice, Colonel Rochester bought land in Dansville including water-power sites on the Canaseraga Creek. Returning north three years later, the three men together bought the 100 acres known as the Allen's Mill Tract in what was then called The Falls. They paid the then-large price of $17.50 per acre.

The Rochester family made quite a procession when in 1810 they journeyed to Dansville. Besides the Colonel, his oldest daughter and five oldest sons rode horses and were followed by his four year-old son on a pet pony. Mrs. Rochester, two more children and some other household members traveled in two carriages, and three wagons pulled by four horses each carried slaves and baggage. That first year in Dansville, by the way, he freed two slaves, a boy sixteen and a girl fourteen. With characteristic enterprise, Rochester built and managed the area's first paper mill and later bought an interest in the carding and cloth-dressing business of William Scott of Scottsburg.

Mr. Scott has written that within Rochester's first year in Dansville he travelled to the Falls every few weeks to survey and lay out lots. "I can see him now," he recalled, "riding up to the door, sitting firmly on a small bay pacing mare and carrying his surveyor's chain and compass strapped to the saddle." He remembered a night when the two shared a room in a tavern, saying, "It was long before sleep visited us, for Colonel Rochester was full of the flattering prospects at the Falls. 'The place must become an important business point,' said he."

Scott also reported that Rochester regretted not having invested all his time and money in the Falls. "Dansville will be a fine village, but the Falls, sir, is capable of great things" were his words. To Scott's protests that he had done much to help Dansville, he answered that he was past the age for building up two towns.

The "building up" of Rochesterville, as it was then called, would have been a large enough undertaking for a man half his years. The contrast between this man's actual age and his youthful energy was accentuated by his looks. Tall and thin, he was, perhaps because of his early illness, considerably stooped, and his face was deeply lined, so that even in the first years of middle-age he looked elderly. Yet in 1811 he wrote with tireless optimism, "I have sold a few lots on Mill, Carroll and Buffalo Streets and have no doubt that a dozen houses will be erected next season."

Selling his Dansville properties three years later, Rochester moved to East Bloomfield where he was able to manage a large farm and still visit Rochesterville often. In 1814 the original 100 acres were divided among the three partners, who each took over the management of his own portion. For the second time in his life, Rochester's neighbors chose him as an elector of the President and Vice-President.

The year 1818 saw the family move to the corner of Exchange and Spring Streets in the city-to-be. A boy who lived next door later wrote of his friendship with Rochester, saying that he visited the older man who worked in his garden early in the mornings "to give him a good appetite for breakfast," as he said. He once observed, "If young people let the sun get the start of them in the morning, they never overtake him during the whole day." Once when planting fruit trees he remarked that he did not know if he would live to eat fruit from them, adding, "But I eat fruit from trees other people planted, so I ought to set out trees for others."

The last of Rochester's many moves was to a home he built on the corner of South Washington and Spring Streets. Enterprising still, he helped establish St. Luke's Church. When Monroe County was formed in 1821, he became its first clerk and first representative in the State Legislature. Having helped found the Bank of Rochester, he was unanimously elected its first president. Because of increasingly poor health, he accepted this office with the understanding that he could resign as soon as the bank was operating well. He resigned within the year, finally admitting that his strength was flagging.

Four years later, however, he supported John Quincy Adams' campaign for the presidency. He died at age seventy-nine after a long illness. A newspaper account said of him, "High nervous energy carried him successfully through enterprises where stronger men might have yielded ... To the last his energy was undiminished." In this respect, he was the prototype of the pioneer Yorker.

SOURCES

Doty, Lockwood L., *A History of Livingston County*
"Rochester, Nathaniel," *Dictionary of American Biography*
Turner, Orsamus, *History of the Pioneer Settlement of Phelps and Gorham's Purchase*

Charles Williamson, Promoter of the Valley

A man who dressed like a courtier, reveled in good food and wine and sponsored horse races on the Genesee flats was hardly a typical Valley settler, but Captain Charles Williamson (1757–1808) was unique. On the other hand, he was the area's first example of what has been called the archetypical American: the businessman. The product that he promoted with New World optimism and enterprise was unsettled land.

A Scotsman, he was sailing to join the British Army in the American Revolution when he was captured at sea and imprisoned in Boston. After his release at the war's end, he married Abigail Newell of Boston, then returned to Scotland. In 1792 he was hired as an agent by Sir William Pulteney, head of British investment company which had recently bought from Robert Morris 1,200,000 acres of land extending from the Pennsylvania border to Lake Ontario. His assignment was to open the area to travel, sell titles and effect improvements.

In June of the same year Williamson and his family arrived in Baltimore. He went from there to Philadelphia and became a naturalized citizen. Then he learned that no road existed into the Genesee country; in fact, he was told that it was impossible to build such a road. By August of 1793, however, he had overseen construction of a road from Pennsylvania through what later became Bath to the point where the Genesee and Canaseraga Rivers meet in what is now Groveland.

Here Captain Williamson began his first settlement, which he named Williamsburg for his employer. He placed an ad in the *Albany Gazette* offering hundreds of thousands of acres for sale at $1 per acre. With characteristic enthusiasm, he wrote, "This is the Country for Peace, Plenty and every luxury the world can afford."

But Williamson's first high hopes were sadly disappointed. A group of Germans sent over by the Pulteney Associates to establish the village proved to have been recruited from among the idlers and ne'er-do-wells of city streets who knew nothing of rural life. Most of them insisted on felling trees with saws, killing several of their number in the process. Those who did wield axes, according to one observer, "made the trees look as if they had been gnawed down by beavers." Despite Williamson's having given them homes, tools and livestock, they refused to work, quarreled and eventually staged a riot from which he barely escaped alive. Thanks to the help of a second group of colonists, who had just arrived the rioters were arrested, tried in the court at Canandaigua and deported to Canada.

Undaunted, this promoter worked to bring about his dream that Williamsburg would grow to be "a place of much trade." Within the first year he had thirty acres cleared and a village of 100 lots laid out around a central square. The principal building was a tavern with a ballroom on the second floor. (Only a few years later this housed a dancing school.) Besides about forty houses, the settlement boasted a church, school, general store, blacksmith shop, distillery, grain warehouse and cemetery. Church services were conducted in the warehouse by the Rev. Samuel J. Mills, father of William Mills, who founded Mt. Morris. A provisional post office brought the community into contact with the outside world.

Nor were such practical accomplishments enough for the imaginative Williamson. As early as 1793 he staged an inspired real estate promotion: "the Williamsburg Fair and Genesee Races." This widely advertized event was for the buying and selling of cattle, horses and sheep. Its gala attraction was a series of horseraces for which Williamson had built a course on the Genesee flats, together with shooting matches and foot races. "As this meeting will be held in the center of a country abounding with provisions," an advertisement stated, "strangers will find no difficulty in providing for themselves and horses." People came from hundreds of miles away, and the event was repeated successfully for several years.

In that same year Captain Williamson began to lay out the town of Bath, which he named in honor of Sir William Pulteney's daughter, the Countess of Bath. Envisioning it as the northern end of a trade route between New York State and Baltimore, he directed the building of a land office, tavern and grist mill. Good roads, sawmills, a church, schools, even a newspaper followed. Though ill with malaria, he built a log cabin to which he brought from Baltimore his wife and children.

It is typical of Charles Williamson that he soon replaced the log cabin with a framed house, planted a garden and brought a gardener from England to tend it. Even when enduring primitive living conditions, he was a dashing figure in his powdered wig, lace cuffs, knee britches and buckled shoes. Said to have been fond of "wine and a good story, of fine horses and sleek cattle," he was an accomplished horseman and a good duelist—all coupled with his business ability.

The Duke de la Rochefoucault-Liancourt, who visited him in 1795, wrote of his "free and easy urbanity," saying,

> We were present at his receiving persons of different ranks and descriptions with whom the apartment he allots to business is generally crowded. He received them all with the same attention, civility and good nature. He ... will even get up from dinner for the sake of dispatching those who wish to speak to him.

The Duke was impressed as well with the Captain's generosity to any newcomers in need. His usual terms for buying land were the obligation to clear a set acreage, to place a family on a farm within eighteen months and to pay half the price after three years and the balance after six.

Williamson had visited the fledgling hamlet of Geneva in Ontario County in 1792, and the next year he had streets and building lots planned. Here he typically combined beauty with practicality. First, the village was to be set on a hill overlooking Seneca Lake, thus removed from malarial swamps below. Second, all houses on the main avenue would face the lake, with no building allowed on the down-hill side of the street to give an unobstructed view of the lake. In 1794 Williamson spent $15,000 to build the Geneva Hotel in a business district he named Pulteney Park. Possibly the finest hotel in the state, its host and chef were from England, and the grand ball celebrating its opening was, to say the least, an anomaly in the wilderness. The developer's more mundane accomplishments included building turnpikes to the Genesee Valley.

In the same year the tireless Williamson established an inn and sold 100 building lots at Sodus Bay on Lake Ontario. This chanced to fan the flames of conflict which had recently been smoldering between New Yorkers and Canadians. Britishers in Canada had lately recruited Indians of Western New York to their cause of regaining that territory. Lieutenant Governor John G. Simcoe sent Williamson a protest against any further colonization of Sodus Bay as constituting a violation of British rights in what he termed "Indian country." Williamson replied that he would ignore Simcoe's threat. George Washington and Gov. George Clinton backed Williamson, and war became a grave possibility. Block houses were built at various sites, including Bath and Canawaugus in Avon. Fortunately, news of General Anthony Wayne's decisive victory over Indians in the West wiped out the Senecas' desire to fight, causing the controversy to blow over. His defiance of the British having increased his popularity, this former captain of the British Army was made a lieutenant colonel of the American forces. Moreover, he was appointed an Ontario County judge in 1795, a Steuben County judge the following year and representative to the State Assembly for both counties after that.

Williamson managed a fair in Bath in 1796, spending $100,000 of the Pulteney Association's money on its attractions, including a theater in which imported actors gave performances each day and night for the better part of a month. Three thousand people came, many bringing their fleetest horses, and saw Williamson's famous mare, Virginia Nell, beaten in a race for a 1,000-pound purse. The celebration brought hundreds of settlers to the region and boosted the price of land first to two and then to four or more dollars an acre. By then, Agent Williamson had returned to his employers an amount equal to their purchase price and all related expenses, plus a net profit of 50,000 pounds sterling.

One negative reaction to Williamson's popularity was expressed in a letter published in the *Wilkesbarre* (Pa.) *Gazette.* Signing himself "A Farmer," the writer complained about his son,

who has been to Bath, the celebrated Bath and has just returned
both a speculator and a gentleman, having spent his money,
swapped away my horse, caught the fever and ague and, what is

infinitely worse that horrid disorder which some call *terra-phobia*.

We can hear nothing from the poor creature now (in his ravings) but of the Captain and Billy—of ranges—townships—numbers—thousands—hundreds—acres—Bath—fairs—races—heats—bets—purses—silk stockings—fortunes—fevers—agues, etc. etc., etc. My son has part of a township for sale . . . It cost him but five dollars per acre; and he was offered six in half a minute after his purchase; but he is positively determined to have eight, besides some precious reserves. One thing is very much in my boy's favor—he has six years' credit. . . . Previous to his late excursion, the lad worked well and was contented at home on my farm; but now work is out of the question with him. There is no managing my boy at home; these golden dreams still beckon him back to Bath, where, as he says, no one need either work or starve; where though a man may have the ague nine months in the year, he may console himself spending the other three fashionably at the races.

When a group of his fellow Scots came to America, Williamson went all the way to Johnstown, N. Y., to persuade them to live on land which was to become Caledonia. Since they were impoverished, he offered them land at only three dollars an acre and promised them provisions until they were self-sufficient, plots for a meeting house and school, help in supporting a minister and money for travel to Caledonia. The canny Scotsmen, unswayed by this largesse until they could inspect the land, sent five men on a 200-mile walk to Caledonia. Happily for all, it met with their approval, and in 1799 twenty-three settlers made the ten-day walk, to be followed by the rest of their party the following spring.

Williamson's success with these "clients" was balanced by a failure with another band of Scots—all because of a poorly-timed joke. The difficulty arose because the visitors were Highlanders, whereas Williamson had come from the Lowlands, there being no love lost between the two groups. Lowlanders were fond of saying that Highlanders often have "the itch." Since this was sometimes the case, sulphur was used to relieve the ailment. Riding with the Highlanders one day as they approached some sulphur springs, the realtor playfully remarked that it would be a good place for them to locate. They were not amused; Williamson lost his sale and the Genesee Valley some solid citizens.

Charles Williamson was indirectly responsible for the founding of Rochester. On his advice, Col. Nathaniel Rochester, who had traveled from Maryland to Williamsburg, bought land in Dansville. At the same time Wiliamson sold 12,000 acres along the Genesee and Caneseraga Rivers to Rochester's companions, Maj. Charles Carroll and Col. William Fitzhugh for two dollars per acre. Three years later the three Southerners bought the 100 acres called the Allan Mills Tract in what was later the City of Rochester. Both Carroll and Fitzhugh brought their families to live near Williamsburg. Southern aristocrats, they introduced an element of plantation-style living to the Valley.

Agent Williamson's good fortune declined when in 1801 Sir William Pulteney, objecting to his extravagant use of the Association's funds, asked him to resign as his agent. Williamson did so, but not before helping to procure a law which allowed aliens to own land in New York State. Williamson had indeed incurred large debts, but during his eight years' work, he had parlayed an initial investment of about $175,000 to more than $3,500,000. Even taking his expenses into account, he had more than doubled the Association's money.

Back in London and separated from his family, Williamson carried out various assignments for the British government. His last venture was a trip to the Spanish West Indies in support of British trade. He was in Havana on his return to London, his mind filled, no doubt, with glorious plans for West Indian land development, when he died of yellow fever.

Williamsburg, which might have been a monument to Charles Williamson, declined and by 1807 was abandoned. Only an unkept graveyard today marks the site of this lost colony. But perhaps it is better to recall the spirit of this dreamer who foresaw great possibilities for Western New York and who wrote of its future:

> Here happy millions their own land possess;
> No tyrant awes them, nor lords oppress.

SOURCES

Brunberg, G. David, *The Making of an Upstate Community, Geneva*
Cowan, Helen I., *Charles Williamson*
Doty, Lockwood L., *History of Livingston County*
McNall, Neil, "The Landed Gentry of the Genesee"
Parker, Arthur C., "Charles Williamson, Builder of the Genesee Country"
"Williamson, Charles," *Dictionary of American Biography*

Williamsburg

The Amazing Adventures of
Moses Van Campen

The Indians having recently been routed from the area, Moses Van Campen (1757–1849) was helping his father work on his farm in Northumberland County, Pennsylvania, one spring day in 1780. It was a rare interval of peace in his life, for he had been engaged in fighting almost continually for the preceding five years. He had left home at age eighteen in 1775 to take part in the Pennamite Wars, a land dispute between Pennsylvania and Connecticut. Later, as an officer in a militia company, he fought both Indians and Tories, surviving several brushes with death. He joined the Continental Army in 1779 and served as both a detachment commander and scout in General Sullivan's campaign against the Iroquois. Once sixteen of his men were killed or wounded around him while he was merely grazed by a bullet. After fighting in the battle of Newtown (now Elmira), he and his men destroyed an Indian village, after which he returned to defending the area of his home.

As Van Campen worked with his father and young brother to repair a barn, they were totally unprepared for the sudden onslaught of marauding Indians, who had captured the rifles of neighboring settlers. Within seconds they killed and scalped the father and boy, wounding Moses slightly and taking him prisoner. The next day they captured two other white men and took the three on a walk to the Genesee Valley.

Van Campen persuaded the others to try to escape. One night, using a knife an Indian had dropped, they cut the ropes binding them and killed nine of their captors. Van Campen threw a tomahawk at the tenth, Chief Mohawk. The weapon struck him in the neck and fell to the ground. The pair then engaged in a violent wrestling match, from which Mohawk ran away.

Returning home once more, Van Campen resumed his defense of Northumberland County settlements. Two years later he and the men in his company of militia were captured: three of them were killed and a fourth saved by Van Campen's risking his own life. They were then taken on a forced march to the Senecas' Council House in Caneadea, Allegany County, New York. Had the Indians known that Van Campen was the man who had injured Mohawk so severely that he carried his head to one side and bore a great scar on his neck, they would have taken pleasure in killing him. Thus he kept his identity to himself.

Along the way to Caneadea, the group met Horatio Jones, also a prisoner who acted as interpreter for Indians and whites. He accidentally learned who Van Campen was and saved his life by pretending ignorance when the Indians quizzed him on the subject. Van Campen later said that Jones's words, "They don't know you," were the happiest he had ever heard.

Even so, the Indians recognized this man as a leader and took special interest in seeing how he would run the gauntlet. They valued bravery so highly that the way a prisoner bore this torture determined how they would treat him later. As the time for his ordeal approached, Van Campen stood at the foot of two lines of Indians extending out from the Council House door. All were eager to strike him with sticks, hatchets, cudgels and whips. Then, running so fast that he had not yet been hit, he saw ahead two young women with whips raised so high that he knew he could not escape their beating. Instantly he formed a plan and, with well-placed kicks and a flying tackle, hurled them both to the ground. The three tumbled about in a confusion of wrestling bodies, a sight so funny to the watching Indians that they broke into hilarious laughter and excitement. As Van Campen's grandson and biographer, the Rev. J. Niles Hubbard, wrote, "He did not wait to help the ladies up," but raced to safety.

"Our hero" was next taken to Fort Niagara and delivered to the British, which he considered preferable to being subjected to the Indians' revenge when they would learn that it was he who had maimed Mohawk. Soon, however, they did find that out and asked Colonel John Butler, chief officer at Niagara, to release Van

Campen to them. After some negotiation, Butler proposed to protect him from their vengeance on the condition that he join the British forces. Scorning almost certain torture and death, Van Campen replied, "No, sir, no! Give me the stake, the tomahawk, or the scalping knife sooner than a British commission!"

As if he had not already exhausted his luck, this adventurer had yet another incredible escape. The wife of a British officer who had known Moses as a schoolmate pleaded with Butler to spare his life. Due to her persuasion, Van Campen was shipped to a prison in Montreal and later sent to Quebec.

Freed at the end of war with the British, he went home but soon returned to duty and took charge of defending Wilkes-Barre Fort. One day he intercepted Ebenezer Allan, the white man called "Indian" Allan, who was traveling to plead with Congress in Washington on behalf of the League of the Iroquois for a peace treaty. To this man, known for his inhuman cruelty, Van Campen said, "Your name is regarded with so much infamy by the inhabitants of the country through which you are to pass on account of your more than savage cruelty . . . that when once they hear of your presence, they will certainly put you to death. That you may go on your business in safety, I will break up my camp and conduct you beyond Wilkes-Barre." With Van Campen's help, Allan completed his mission safely.

After retiring from the Army, Van Campen married the daughter of a wealthy man, farmed his land and learned surveying. In 1796 the couple and their five daughters were among the first settlers of Almond in Allegany County, New York. Another move took them to nearby Angelica where Philip Church hired the former soldier to survey his 100,000-acre tract, and the two became lifelong friends. Besides serving as elder of the Presbyterian Church, Van Campen was appointed successively a judge of the Court of Common Pleas, justice of the peace, county treasurer and deputy county clerk.

During these years Indians often came from their village of Caneadea to visit him. One day Van Campen was conversing with Chief Shongo (whose son married a daughter of Mary Jemison) when the two learned that they had fought in the same skirmish of the battle of Newtown. Van Campen described wounding an Indian when the man had to re-load his gun, to which Shongo exclaimed, "I same Indian," and showed a scar which substantiated the encounter.

In 1831 the Major moved to Dansville where he headed the party which surveyed the original village boundaries. He also helped survey the village property of the Revolutionary War hero, Capt. William Perine, who, besides naming two streets for his first and last names, named another Van Campen. A member of the Presbyterian Church, Moses contributed to a fund to buy books for its Sunday School. He liked to sit in the general store and recount his exploits. He and Gen. William Mills of Mt. Morris often exchanged visits, and he and Horatio Jones visited each other once a year, occasionally drinking grog on the steps of a tavern and regaling an audience with their daring deeds. It was Jones who persuaded Chief Mohawk to call on his former foe. "He will not want to see me," the chief demurred.

"It is peace now," Jones replied. "He will be glad to see you." Mohawk's knock on Van Campen's door was answered by his daughter. Quite frightened, she reported to her father, who was ill in bed, that a man she thought was Mohawk wanted to see him. Van Campen instructed her to let him in and, when Mohawk said who he was, told him to come closer to the bed. Feeling the scar on the chief's neck, he exclaimed, "Yes, you are Mohawk. That's my mark!" From then on, the two were friends, and as a token of reconciliation Mohawk carved a wooden ladle and gave it to Van Campen's daughter. One time her husband, knowing well the full story, asked Mohawk with pretended innocence how he came by the scar. All Mohawk would say on the subject was "Yankee done it. Yankee done it. Peace now."

In 1841 patriotic citizens honored the memories of Lt. Thomas Boyd and Sgt. Michael Parker, members of Sullivan's expedition, by removing their remains to the new Mt. Hope cemetery in Rochester. Chosen to preside at ceremonies in Cuylerville was the eighty-four-year-old Van Campen, one of the area's three surviving veterans of Sullivan's army. In the name of Livingston County, he ceremoniously handed over his former comrades' relics for respectful burial.

Van Campen asked that the Rev. Thomas Aitken of Sparta might preach at his own burial, which occurred in 1849. He would have liked the sermon text: "I have fought the good fight."

SOURCES

Bunnell, A. O., ed., *Dansville 1789-1902*
DeLong, H. W., Sr., *Boyhood Reminiscences With Other Sketches*
Doty, Lockwood L., *History of Livingston County*
History of Allegany County, N. Y.
Hubbard, J. Niles, *Sketches of Border Adventures in the Life and Times of Major Moses Van Campen*
Peer, Sherman, "The Genesee River Country: Historical Sketches"
Phelan, Helene C., *Allegany's Uncommon Folk*
Sheer, Hazel M., *Tales from Allegany County*

Major Moses Van Campen

The Tragedy of Red Jacket

Horatio Jones called Red Jacket (1758–1830) the greatest man that ever lived. He reasoned that other leaders had become outstanding thanks to their educational advantages, whereas, if this Seneca Indian had had similar privileges, he woud have surpassed them. Such speculation aside, Red Jacket was, with Corn Planter, one of the two great Seneca chiefs, a powerful orator and gifted political leader. Unfortunately, his passionate beliefs were out of step with his times. He was an unwelcome prophet.

This man was called by three names. Recognizing his native ability when he was a boy of ten, his elders named him Otetiani, meaning "Always Ready." While a messenger for the British at Niagara, he was given a red military coat and thus the nickname, Red Jacket. Then because he belonged to the Wolf clan, the adult Indian name bestowed on him was Sagoyewatha. Referring to a wolf's howling, it means "He keeps them awake," and it had the double reference of the young man's spellbinding oratory.

Red Jacket was caught in the clash of Iroquois and white cultures. He saw the Colonists' war against the British divide the League of the Iroquois, with Indians fighting on both sides. Sullivan's devastation of Little Beard's Town embittered him, especially because Indians considered it a sacrilege to destroy growing food. Nor could any Indians understand the white man's beliefs that their "discovery" of the New World gave them title to it and that they were destined by God to conquer the territory.

Even sadder, Red Jacket was his own worst enemy. A streak of vanity made him court popularity with both his own people and the whites and to shift his stand on political issues to please the crowd. He bitterly opposed the Indians' sale of their land, yet several times signed such treaties after they were made. He resisted the intrusion of European civilization into native life, such as the Washington government's effort to persuade Indians to exchange hunting for large-scale farming. In 1792, however, he accepted Washington's gift of a large silver medal showing the two sharing a pipe of peace and in the background a man plowing the land.

Red Jacket's less worthy traits came to the fore during negotiations for the Treaty of the Big Tree. When in 1793 William Morris sold that part of New York State west of the Genesee River to the Holland Land Company, he contracted to extinguish the Indians' title to it. It was not until 1797 that the Senecas consented to consider the matter, at which time Thomas Morris acting for his father and Col. Jeremiah Wadsworth of Connecticut representing the United States government met with them in what is now Geneseo.

As a civil chief, Red Jacket argued vehemently against selling the land for any price, while others favored the sale. When, after two weeks the discussions reached an impasse, Morris threatened to end them. To his consternation, Red Jacket acted on the suggestion, putting out the council fire. Morris then presented the women of the tribe with beads and trinkets and promised life-long annuities to those chiefs who would comply with the sale.

This led to a revolt by the women and warrior chiefs which overturned the authority of the civil chiefs, for it was Seneca tradition that the land belonged to the women who tilled it and the warriors who defended it, and these two groups could override the civil chiefs in property negotiations. Once again the Indians had been divided and conquered. All of New York State west of the Genesee went for two and one-half cents an acre.

At this Red Jacket became drunk until the council was ended. He confided to Morris that he had no objections to the land sale and had pretended otherwise only to maintain his prestige with the civil chiefs. Publicly he refused to sign the treaty; privately he arranged to have space left at the head of the listed signatures, so that his, when filled in later, would show his prominence. He also obtained not only an annuity of one hundred dollars for life, but also a cash payment six times larger than that given any other chief.

This difficult man had a true friend in Horatio Jones, the captive-turned-interpreter, whom he is said to have adopted as his son. Many were the times when Jones took care of the drunken orator. One time when he had breakfast with the Jones family, Mrs. Jones played a little joke on him. Knowing that he took a large amount of sugar in his coffee, she fixed his without any. "My son," Red Jacket demanded of Jones, "do you let your squaw trifle thus with your father?" When the suppressed laughter of the Jones children showed that they were in on the trick, he asked again, "And do you allow your children to make sport of their chief?" Apologies were necessary; Mrs. Jones handed over the sugar bowl; Red Jacket testily filled his cup to the brim with sugar.

With his thorough knowledge of the Seneca language, Jones was probably the only white man who could appreciate Red Jacket's oratorical skill. He often spoke of his phenomenal memory and eloquence. One example is his plea on behalf of Tommy Jemmy, a chief who had been responsible for the execution of an Indian woman found guilty of witchcraft in 1821. Since witchcraft was no longer the custom of white people, they tried Jemmy for murder. Red Jacket defended him in trial after trial up to the court of last resort. "What," he thundered to the court,

> do you denounce us as fools and bigots because we still believe that which you yourselves believed two centuries ago? . . .
>
> Go to Salem! Look at the records of your own government and you will find that hundreds have been executed for the crime which has called forth the sentence of execution against this woman and drawn down upon her the arm of vengeance.
>
> What have our brothers done more than the rulers of your people? And what crime has this man committed by executing in a summary way the laws of his country and the command of the Great Spirit?

Tommy Jemmy was acquitted.

Red Jacket became increasingly opposed to the inroads of white men's ways into the Indians' lives. As he saw his people's culture decline, he fought to isolate them from new influences. He was especially bitter about Christian missionaries. "We are few and weak," he contended, "but may for a long time be happy if we hold fast to our country and the religion of our forefathers." But no one could resist the inevitable changes and losses which the future held for the Indians.

By 1827 habitual drunkenness had eroded Red Jacket's ability;

28

his objections to "progress" had cost him popularity; and his wife and children had turned against him to become Christians. He was deposed as a chief, but later, thanks to his eloquent defense of his actions, was restored to that rank. In old age he somewhat moderated his hatreds, except for his unrelenting objection to the loss of Indian lands.

Had he been as wise as he was passionate, more flexible and tolerant, he might possibly have changed the fate of the Senecas. As it was, he mourned at his life's end, "My heart fails me when I think of my people, who are soon to be scattered and forgotten."

SOURCES

Farrington, Frank, "He That Keeps Them Awake"
Harris, George, *The Life of Horatio Jones*
Hubbard, J. Niles, *An Account of Sagoyewatha, or Red Jacket and His People*
Kenway, Mary M. "Portraits of Red Jacket"
Kolecki, John H., *Red Jacket, the Last of the Senecas*
Parker, Arthur C., *Red Jacket, Last of the Seneca*
"Red Jacket," *Dictionary of American Biography*
Stone, William, *The Life and Times of Sa-Go-Ye-Wat-Ha or Red Jacket*

A Postscript to the Boyd and Parker Killing

There is a little-known sequel to the story of the torture and killing of the Revolutionary soldiers, Lt. Thomas Boyd and Sgt. Michael Parker (both?–1779). In 1779 Gen. John Sullivan's army under orders from George Washington laid waste the Senecas' land in the Valley in order to force them onto the care of the British at Fort Niagara. A scouting party at what is now Groveland was caught in an ambush and its fifteen members killed except Lieutenant Boyd and Sergeant Parker.

Taken to Little Beard's Town (Cuylerville), the two were prisoners of Joseph Brant, chief of the Indian party. Besides having once attended what later became Dartmouth College, he had gone to London and there joined the Masonic Order. Legend has it that Lieutenant Boyd, knowing this, gave him a secret sign of brotherhood, which Brant acknowledged with the implied promise of mercy to his captives. Unfortunately, Brant was called away, leaving Maj. John Butler in command.

According to local lore, Butler and Little Beard then directed acts of unspeakable cruelty. They lashed Parker with whips, then cut off his head and beheaded Boyd as well but only after acts of extreme torture. (There is evidence that this event may be legendary, the atrocity having been shifted in the telling from another time and place to this one; in any case, Boyd's and Parker's remains lay in unmarked, though not unknown, graves.)

Sixty-two years later in 1841, Professor Samuel Treat, principal of Temple Hill Academy in Geneseo, said in a July Fourth oration that it was shameful that no monument honored the fallen soldiers. When the Rochester papers took up the matter, some citizens conceived the idea of exhuming their remains and transferring them to the new Mt. Hope Cemetery. There a plot named Revolutionary Hill would be set aside for the re-burial of all "the gallant seventy-sixers" of the Valley and a monument erected to their undying honor.

Henry O'Reilly, Rochester newspaper editor, was one who held meetings to urge this plan onto the citizens of Groveland and Cuylerville. Despite some opposition to the fact that the remains were being taken from Livingston County, consent was obtained from a majority of those who took the trouble to attend the meetings. A two-part ceremony was planned to be held first in Cuylerville, later in Rochester. As a veteran of Sullivan's Campaign, the eighty-five-year-old Maj. Moses Van Campen was chosen to preside at exercises marking the removal of the patriots' remains. Gov. William Seward consented to preside at the reburial.

The ceremony began with the arrival in Cuylerville of a flotilla of five boatloads of Rochester dignitaries coming down the canal. Judge George Hosmer of Avon had been scheduled to give the major address but, shortly before the appointed day, had announced that he was too old and infirm to speak. The task fell to Professor Treat, who hurriedly briefed himself on Boyd's and Parker's fate. At the last minute while riding to Cuylerville in a carriage with Van Campen, he borrowed the Major's notes and found that he had to correct some errors in his speech. Nevertheless, it was reported that he spoke "in a strain of eloquence and manly feeling highly honorable to him as a historian and scholar." To the accompaniment of dirges played by a military band, an urn containing bones and some pewter uniform buttons was handed over.

In Rochester Governor Seward was so late in arriving from an appointment in Buffalo that a long line of carriages and a crowd of pedestrians were forced to wait for him at the cemetery gates. When he did appear, his first words on meeting Professor Treat were, "Post me! Post me on what is happening!" Treat instead began to introduce him to one of the three surviving veterans of Sullivan's army who were present. But this man happened to be a bitter political opponent of the governor. "What, Seward?" he cried out in disgust. "Small Potatoes Bill? I don't want to know him!" Treat was embarrassed; Seward thought it funny.

The many orations were just finished but the urn not yet buried when the skies let down a cloudburst, sending the crowd running for cover. This later gave rise to claims that the urn never was buried and had been vandalized. A *Rochester Republican* editor went so far as to claim that the urn held not patriots' remains but the bones of a bear. The controversy raged in letters to newspapers for years with bitter feeling on both sides. No monument was erected; what was to have been Revolutionary Hill was leveled in 1864 and bones found there put in the cemetery's potters' field.

Samuel Treat liked to tell a postscript to this story. Several years afterward he was in Washington and went to the Senate chambers to hear Seward speak. "He had only to open his mouth and let it run," Treat interpolated. "Webster, Douglas, Mangum and others were standing around, not paying much attention." When Seward finished, he walked toward Treat, did not recognize him for a moment, then said, "Oh, you are one of the fellows who got me up to Rochester to orate over the bear's bones!"

After a lapse of sixty-two years, what may or may not have been the soldiers' remains were re-buried once again. Two members of the Irondoquoit chapter of the Daughters of the American Revolution, having found Revolutionary soldiers' remains in the cemetery "poor grounds," had them moved to a plot marked by a boulder and plaque. In 1903 the elderly widow of Samuel Treat, members of the Daughters and Sons of the American Revolution and others held a solemn burial service at a plot overlooking the Genesee River. It was arranged for this site to have perpetual care. As to that, time will tell.

SOURCES

Livingston County Historical Society, *Annual Report, 1904*

The Wadsworths of Geneseo 1790–1864

"I met Mr. (James) Wadsworth, who has settled in the Geneseo country . . . and who I find . . . is in raptures with it. Mr. Wadsworth is extremely intelligent and one upon whose veracity the utmost reliance can be placed." In these words Robert Morris cited three leading characteristics of James Wadsworth (1768–1844): enthusiasm for the Valley, intelligence and integrity. His brother, William, (1761–1833) shared these same traits, although his intelligence was less sophisticated.

The Wadsworth brothers also had youth, ambition and a desire for adventure when in June of 1790 they left their favored social position in Durham, Connecticut, to explore the little-known Genesee Country. From their uncle, Jeremiah Wadsworth, they bought part of the Big Tree Tract, which he had purchased from Oliver Phelps and Nathaniel Gorham, and agreed to be agents for the sale of the rest of his tract of some 4,000 acres.

Traveling separately, James took provisions by boat, and William drove an oxcart loaded with several hired men, a Negro woman slave and necessities for survival. They met in Canandaigua where they bought cattle. The road ahead of them had to be cleared so often that they made only about twelve miles' progress each day. After parting at the foot of Conesus Lake, James temporarily lost the obscure trail to Big Tree (Geneseo) but soon found his way there at night by the light of a candle which the slave, Jenny, held as William began splitting logs to build a cabin.

After clearing the land, the brothers planted a few crops. From the first, they were pleased with their prospects, James writing home, " . . . all accounts confirm us in our choice. All hands are in good health and fine spirits. . . . We expect many difficulties but are fast in the belief that perseverance will surmount them."

By September, however, William was laid low with malaria, as were the hired men, who soon departed for the healthier air of Connecticut. James, too, wintered there in order to develop contacts for land sales, leaving only William and Jenny to care for the stock. Returning to the Valley the next summer, James found that William had made an enclosed pasture and raised promising crops of wheat, corn and hay. Admitted to the practice of law in Ontario County, James began to sell lots to people migrating west. To grind their wheat, the brothers built a mill at Conesus in 1792.

They were still living in their log house when the Duke de la Rochefoucault Liancourt came visiting three years later. Offended by their primitive home, he wrote, "Their house is as dirty as any I have ever seen. It stank so I could hardly bear it." His stay was further marred when his pet poodle, Cartouche, killed one of Jenny's chickens, and she expressed her opinion of French dukes and dogs in unflattering terms. The next morning, as William prepared to leave for a muster of the militia which he commanded, Jenny dressed his hair for the occasion. This doughty woman deserves more than a footnote in Valley annals for having so faithfully helped the brothers in those first years as well as once having saved James's life. While the Wadsworths' relations with the Indians were good on the whole, the Indians resented their having felled many trees and gave James a name meaning "killer of trees." A group of drunken Indians once came to kill him on this account, but Jenny, who understood the Seneca language, knew their plan and hid James under several covers of ticking. The Indians jabbed their knives into this without harming him.

The years 1796–1798 saw James tour Europe on behalf of a group of American financiers with the hope of selling land to foreign investors, at the same time extending his agency for the sale of more land. This left William with the responsibility for expanding their farming operation, which now consisted of about 2,000 cleared acres, much of it rented to tenants. He raised cattle to sell in Philadelphia and Baltimore and grew corn and tobacco as well as hemp, which he manufactured into rope.

Obviously, the brothers worked out a division of duties according to their contrasting personalities. A Yale graduate, a sometime schoolteacher and a lawyer, James was the more bookish and cosmopolitan and perhaps had the greater social conscience. "Old Bill," as he was called from his youth, was said to care for nothing but fighting and farming. Six feet tall, slender and handsome in a rough-cut way, he was a commanding figure on his magnificant black charger. He was at ease with people of all classes, and whenever his backwoods neighbors held what the historian, Orsamus Turner, has termed "a rude frolic," he was one of them. While James was in Europe, Bill built them a cobblestone house.

By the turn of the century, the Wadsworths owned 34,500 acres reaching from Geneseo to Chili and Henrietta, most of it leased by settlers. One of James's methods to persuade New England families to settle in Genesee Country was to accept their land in the East as payment and then sell it. It may have been on such a visit that he met Naomi Wolcott of East Windsor, Connecticut, whom he married in 1804.

His travels in England had fostered in him a desire for a large and beautiful country estate; the Home Farm sloping from the south end of Geneseo down to the river was as charming a site as any he had seen. There he built The Homestead for his bride. A two-story wooden building in the Federal style, its columned entrance faced meadows to the east, and a terrace on the west side gave an even finer view across the Valley. A visitor to The Homestead during Naomi Wadsworth's management wrote, " . . . under circumstances that all who have attempted housekeeping on a liberal scale in new settlements will know to be difficult, the mansion at Geneseo became a model of well-ordered, generous and yet unostentatious hospitality."

From their first years in the Valley, the Wadsworths practiced tenant farming. Whereas this "lease-hold" system has created great injustices in other times and places, there was, for many years, no shortage of willing tenants for Wadsworth land, since the arrangement worked well for both renters and owners. The reason seems to lie within the special provisions of the brothers' contracts. It was agreed that the tenant would first clear and fence the land and build a house and barn, in return for which he would be given free use of the land for a certain number of years. After that, the tenant would pay rent of a prescribed number of bushels of wheat delivered at the Wadsworths' mill. In general, the tenant agreed to cultivate his farm in a "good and farmerlike manner; to commit no waste, nor suffer any to be committed." An important factor of the relationship was that the tenant paid all taxes on his lot; this attracted steady workers who intended to remain on their farms for some years. The historian, Neil McNall, has explained that this form of tenancy succeeded because of:

> the community of interest between men with land which they wished to retain, but from which they wished to derive revenue, and men who wished to secure land to till and did not regard ownership as an indispensable feature of their tenure.

Furthermore, James and William farmed their own acres on the same footing as their tenants, doing menial labor when it was necessary. They could supervise the operation of adjoining tenant farms as absentee landlords never could. Stipulated in every tenant's contract were enlightened conservation methods, which the brothers themselves practiced. When they had first cleared the land, they left clumps of great trees standing in the fields, and tenants were not allowed to cut any of these. Crops were to be rotated; the "dung clause" required that all manure produced by stock on a farm be expended on it. As the writer, Sherman Peer, has said, "To the would-be aristocrats of the land in Colonial days, the land was a servant; to generations of Wadsworths, it was a partner, the same as to a husband and wife on a family-sized farm." In the long run, this far-sighted view benefited both parties. In addition, James and Bill introduced to the Valley advanced farming methods such as importing superior animals for breeding stock, including Merino sheep.

They were not invariably prosperous, however. From time to time they were "land poor"—crop failures, Genesee fever, land buyers defaulting on debts and the War of 1812 caused hardship. As a leader of the area militia, Bill was made major general in the War of 1812. He fought in the Battle of Queenstown, as a nephew reported, "with his right arm broke (sic) and his sword in his left hand." He was seriously wounded and taken prisoner but released later.

From the first, the Wadsworths contributed to community improvements. James had said that he would give 100 acres to the first regularly incorporated religious society in Geneseo and redeemed the promise to the Geneseo Gospel Society (Central Presbyterian Church) in 1816. In 1820 both gave land for a common school. The brothers' gift of land for a courthouse and jail was one of the reasons why Geneseo became the county seat when Livingston County was formed in 1821. Bill was one of the town's first assessors and a county supervisor for twenty-one years.

Public education, especially as it had practical use, was James's chief concern. In his opinion, "the man who is instructed is a double man." As early as 1876, he urged that common schools be established throughout New York State. Then, seeing that money to build schools was largely wasted when they were taught by lamentably ignorant men, he took up the cause of teacher-training. Besides much letter writing and the financing of lectures and pamphlets, he influenced the Commissioners of Education to promote the Lancaster system. This was a then-innovative system whereby a teacher first taught the ablest students, then had each of them teach a group of students. James was elected Geneseo's Commissioner of Common Schools in 1816 and two years later an inspector.

The brothers jointly gave two acres of land for the Livingston County High School (Temple Hill Academy). Both were among the subscribers of additional funds, and James donated its buildings. This school provided more advanced teaching than did the common schools and aimed to "combine classical instruction with that of the useful arts—and at a moderate expense." With characteristic practicality, James wrote, "It will be no injury to a mason to become acquainted with the properties of air, nor to a millwright with the properties of fluids, and, I add, to the mighty mass of mind throughout the State to reason correctly." He also wrote of this school, "If our institutions are to be preserved, the sons of the rich man and of the poor man ought to be educated in the same seminary. They will both be the better from early associations."

Ten years later James would finance the publication of two books on education and support the State's purchase of books for school libraries. Himself the owner of a fine library, he would in 1841 underwrite the cost of the Geneseo Atheneum, forerunner of Geneseo's Wadsworth Library. This was a library of books, scientific equipment and mineral specimens primarily for use by Livingston County High School students but also "open and free for the gratuitous use of the inhabitants of the County of Livingston." Since subscription libraries were then the rule, this was a far-sighted exception.

Sorrow came to the family when Naomi and her daughter,

Cornelia, died in 1831, followed two years later by the deaths of another daughter, Harriet, and William Wadsworth. After her mother's death, Elizabeth Wadsworth (1815-1851) was hostess for her father. The youngest of five children, she had grown to be called "the lily of the Valley," and her portrait by Sully shows a beautiful young woman.

When Elizabeth was twenty, Hon. Charles Augustus Murray, an aristocratic young Englishman, visited her father and won her heart. Murray has been described as "exceedingly handsome and agreeable with a strong taste for literature and an excellent classical scholar." His scholarly bent must have been balanced by a love of fun, for when an Oxford student, he bet he could ride the sixty miles to London and back in one day. Using three relays of horses, he and a friend rode there, took a ride in a park, dined at a club, saw the first act of a play and returned to their lodgings at three minutes before midnight.

Murray and Elizabeth wanted to marry, but her father forbade it because of his memories of warfare with the British. Continuing his original plan to see America, Murray traveled west where he lived with a wandering tribe of Pawnee Indians for three months. He later incorporated the exciting adventures and narrow escapes of this experience in a book entitled *Travels in North America.*

The couple must have thought that their future happiness was assured when, on Murray's return visit a year later, James Wadsworth consented to their engagement. A few months afterward, however, he withdrew his permission, forbidding them even to write one another, and Murray returned to England. In defense of Wadsworth's tyranny, it should be remembered that he had recently experienced the deaths of four of those dearest to him; perhaps the thought of losing the company of the lovely Elizabeth was more than he could bear. Always a reserved man, he was becoming austere with advancing age.

Charles and Elizabeth refrained from corresponding with each other. As the dutiful daughter, she continued to be mistress of The Homestead. Her letters show that she had some happy times. "We had quite a gay day for Geneseo," she wrote of New Year's Day of 1839. "Many of the villagers called, also the whole fire company *en masse,* and a number of young swains whom I took particularly to myself. We had quite a merry day." Later she described a ball at The Homestead:

Our rooms were filled with a group of as well-dressed, well-behaved mortals as ever graced the most aristocratic house in Boston!!! We had most excellent music, three violins and a trombone, took up the carpet in the dining room ... Tom Newbold and LeRoy were in the best possible spirits. The latter danced all evening and jumped about like other folks.

In 1844 Murray wrote a story, "The Prairie Bird," in which he indirectly assured Elizabeth that he still loved her. That was the year of James Wadsworth's death, after which Charles proposed again. But this time she refused. She felt that at twenty-eight she was too old to be attractive—that he was merely asking out of pity.

Yet four years later, a visitor described her in glowing terms, writing:

She is a remarkable person ... She is young, handsome, intellectual, cultivated, graceful and elegant, of most lovely pure and elevated character, living alone in the country and managing her own household and estate. She has frequently passed whole winters entirely alone, her brother's family being in New York or Philadelphia. It implies great intellectual resources and some powerful secret cause, that such a woman of such quick and sensitive feelings as she can lead such a life. She says she prefers it and is satisfied, that her library and garden are sufficient for her ...

In 1848 Elizabeth gave the Village of Geneseo the land in front of The Homestead, which had formerly been the village square but was by then neglected. She had it enclosed with a handsome railing, planted trees on it, giving it as a park in perpetuity.

But even with all her inner resources, Elizabeth must have wanted a vacation, and the year 1850 saw her traveling with friends to England. By a coincidence that no writer of fiction would dare attempt, the train they chanced to ride stopped at a station where into her compartment stepped none other than Charles Augustus Murray! They were engaged within a week and married in six months. From England they went to Cairo where he was the British Consul General. The next year a son was born to them, and lovely Elizabeth died in childbirth.

If The Homestead is seen as a gatepost at the south end of Geneseo's short Main Street, its north end is marked by Hartford

House, home of James Samuel Wadsworth (1807–1864), the eldest son of the pioneer, James. It is unfortunate that Naomi did not live to see the man her son later became, for shortly before her death, young Samuel was a pleasure-loving gallant. No great student, he was expelled from Harvard for an infraction of discipline. He then read law in Daniel Webster's office, which he followed by brief study at Yale Law School and an Albany law firm. In 1834 he married Mary Craig Wharton of Philadelphia, who was said to be even more beautiful than her sister-in-law, Elizabeth, and was once described as "the most beautiful woman in the country and as agreeable and accomplished as beautiful."

On their wedding trip to Europe, the couple obtained the plans of the villa of Lord Hertford in London and in 1835–1837 built Hartford House as a replica. A combination of Colonial Georgian and Greek Revival styles, its three-story central unit is extended on each side by one-story wings and two-story units. Built of brick later covered with stucco, the mansion had a portico on both front and rear sides. Sidney G. Fisher, the gentleman who provided the admiring description of Elizabeth, thought it the finest estate in America, "like a gentleman's house of the best description in town." He wrote of its setting that it was:

> situated in a park of about 400 acres and commanding an extensive view of the magnificent flats, most of which belong to him. . . . It is a beautiful piece of ground in very rich pasture and covered with groves and clumps of trees. From the back of the house the view over this ground and the extensive flats is superb
> . . .

Hartford House was where James began to take life more seriously. Here he fattened steers and raised beef cattle on the 2,000-acre Home Farm besides overseeing the tenant farming. Here too the couple raised six children and extended lavish hospitality to their many friends, including President Van Buren's son, John, and Charles Sumner, the abolitionist senator. One year saw the entire family tour Europe in a massive carriage, and it was during this trip that they visited their son, Charles, and his companion, Henry Ward, in Paris. Generous to a fault, James gave large sums to charity and sent enough grain to fill an entire ship to victims of the Irish famine in 1847. Once the Geneseo authorities stopped local Roman Catholics from their practice of holding services in the courthouse at a time when Wadsworth was out of town. Thus on his return he questioned why he saw people kneeling on the porch of a small home where Mass was being celebrated; learning the reason, he gave land for a church and a $500 loan, payable at the parish's convenience. His contributions to the town included the public water system, fire-fighting equipment and the use of land for Agricultural Society fairs. When Valley wheat-growers were ruined by infestation of the wheat midge, Wadsworth took only so much rent from his tenants as they could afford after providing for their families. Also James had the responsibility of caring for the widow and three sons of his brother, William Wolcott, as well as looking after the inheritances of the children of his sisters, Harriet and Elizabeth.

Since the days of his friendship with the Van Burens, James had been ardently interested in politics. In 1848 some Democrats nominated him for governor, but he withdrew in favor of John Dix. His anti-slavery sentiments led to his presiding at a convention of Democrat-Republicans, a group opposed to the extension of slavery. Again he was asked to run for the governorship but refused in favor of Governor Morgan. A Lincoln supporter, he was chosen a presidential elector three times.

As war loomed on the horizon in 1861, Wadsworth represented New York State at a peace conference which tried to save the Union despite the fact that he was inalterably opposed to any compromise on the urgent need to overthrow slavery. At a local political meeting that year, he said, "If war is to come, as I fear it must, I want it to come in my day when I am able to bear my share in the ordeal and not have it left over as a bitter legacy for my children."

With the surrender of Fort Sumter in April, James S. Wadsworth's destiny was sealed. As a member of the Union Defense Committee of New York, he sent a boatload of provisions to Union troups under siege. He was soon appointed to the staff of General Irwin McDowell in Virginia. In July he led the charge of the 13th infantry in the Battle of Bull Run, staying on the field after the Union defeat to care for the wounded and see to burial of the dead. The next month he was made a brigadier general in command of the First New York Brigade. Later made Military Governor of Washington, he enjoyed the friendship of Lincoln and his secretary, John Hay. Once again nominated for Governor, Wadsworth ran on an abolitionist slate but lost because many New Yorkers were luke-warm about abolishing slavery. His defeat, however, resulted in his being granted his wish to go to the front. When Wadsworth once stood erect among men ordered to lie flat while crossing a river in a small boat, an observer remarked, "General Wadsworth will never see the end of this war—he's too brave a man." The death of a general at the Battle of Gettysburg made Wadsworth the senior officer of his brigade, and he fought valiantly. During an interim in the fighting, Lincoln commissioned Wadsworth to recruit Negro regiments. Then when General Grant was made Commander in Chief of the U.S. Army, Wadsworth, now a major general, applied for active duty and was given command of a division which consisted of the former First Division and his Iron Brigade. The Battle of the Wilderness was another terrible defeat for the Union in which, while riding to within feet of enemy fire, General James S. Wadsworth was struck by a bullet and killed.

It may be that he was one whom Lincoln recalled when he wrote, "that from these honored dead we take increased devotion to the cause for which they gave the last full measure of devotion—that we here highly resolve that these dead shall not have died in vain."

SOURCES

Barraco, Anthony M., "The Wadsworth Family of New York"
Denison, Frances, Scrapbook
Fisher, Sidney G., "A Philadelphia Perspective" in *Diary 1834-1871*
Hatch, Alden, *The Wadsworths of the Genesee*
McNall, Neil, "The First Half-Century of Wadsworth Tenancy"
Parker, Kathleen, "The Wadsworths' Political and Public Service Contributions to the United States"
Pearson, Henry G., *James S. Wadsworth of Geneseo, New York*
Peer, Sherman, "The Genesee River Country: Historical Sketches"
Renwick, James, "Life of James Wadsworth"
Turner, Orsamus, *History of the Pioneer Settlement of Phelps and Gorham's Purchase*
Winkelman, John H., "The Wadsworth Library (1869-1955) in the Genesee Valley"

Horatio Jones, "Handsome Boy"

Handsome Boy is the name the Senecas gave their captive, Horatio Jones (1763–1844), one woman saying that he was the handsomest person, white or red, her people had ever seen. Raised in Downington, Pennsylvania, he was expert in riding, shooting, wrestling and running. He worked in his father's gunsmith shop and became a skilled marksman. In 1777 at age fourteen, he served as a fifer in a company of minute men; at sixteen he was a scout for the Bedford Rangers; the next year he ran away from home to join them on a foray against Indians.

On a march into Indian territory one foggy morning, the company was trapped in an ambush. Jones tried to run to safety, but, falling down when his moccasin thong caught in a shrub, he felt sure he was doomed. Instead, he heard a friendly voice say, "No be scairt, me no hurt you. You very nice boy; you run like deer. You make fine Indian boy. Me good friend, me help you." This was a half-white, half-Indian man called Jack Berry, whom a Seneca woman had asked to choose a captive to replace her son killed in battle. She had given Berry a wampum belt bearing her clan totem and family mark, which he placed around Horatio's neck.

During an agonizing forced march when Jones saw many of his fellow-prisoners tortured and killed, he gained the Senecas' respect by feigning indifference to hunger, fatigue and outrage. One day when a deer had been killed some distance from the party's camp, Jones was told to go with other youths to bring it back. He set off on a run and happened to race beside the Senecas' fastest runner. This man had been a runner for British officers at Fort Niagara, who called him Sharp Shins because he ran so fast that his shins cut the air. Reaching the deer ahead of Sharp Shins, Horatio clearly showed he had no intention of escaping and won the admiring comment, "The handsome boy is a fast runner. He runs like the wind." At the same time, however, he won the hatred of Sharp Shins.

After that Handsome Boy was treated more leniently than the other prisoners. But he learned that he had one more ordeal to endure: he had to run the gauntlet. This was a ritual in which prisoners ran through a double line of assailants to atone for their people's wrongs to the Indians. It gave those who had not been among the war party a chance for revenge. It was also the final test of endurance for any captives slated for adoption.

Jones stood on the bank of the Genesee River in Caneadea, which he must ford before racing through the gauntlet to the safety of the Seneca council house. He watched the women and young men line up for the attack, heard their whoops, knew all too well the meaning of their tomahawks, knives, whips, clubs and stones. At the last minute Jack Berry whispered to him the trick of running the gauntlet successfully. He was to follow very close behind the next to last runner and keep so near one line of attackers that they would have neither time nor room to strike him. Jones followed directions and, spattered with the blood and brains of the man before him, whose head was sliced off, he reached the council house door—only to find his way barred by none other than Sharp Shins, his tomahawk held aloft.

Darting aside and racing around the house, the captive heard Sharp Shin's tomahawk whirl an inch past his head. Since he found no other door to the house, he ran down a path to the woods. There, a woman and her daughter sitting before their house jumped up, pulled him inside and hid him under a bed. His adoptive mother, recognizing the wampum around his neck, knew him as her new son.

Later the Indians sat in council to hear Jack Berry tell of his commission to bring back a son for a bereaved mother and all that followed. To this, Chief Shongo replied that the Great Spirit had sent this handsome boy for a good purpose, that he would become one of them and that the future would show why he had been given to them. Horatio thus became the son of Chief Cornplanter's sister and her husband, whose name meant "Great Hunter." As he was usually referred to as "the handsome boy," he was given the Indian name with that meaning.

Coming to terms with life as a Seneca, Hoc-sa-go-wah gave up any plan for escape. He became fluent in the language and soon served as an interpreter. In his work of questioning white captives he had the delicate task of both pleasing his "family" and sparing white prisoners from vicious retaliation at the same time. In addition he gradually took on the jobs of gunsmith, blacksmith and silversmith.

He learned that maintaining a stance of bravery at all times earned his fellows' respect. He also sensed the importance of ignoring physical hardships, of consistently telling the truth and of doing his fair share of work. At the same time, he never accepted an insult. One time a group of young braves, egged on by Sharp Shins, tried to test his patience. When one of them went too far, he thrust a boiling-hot squash down the tormentor's shirt—to the delight of all bystanders. Another time Sharp Shins threw a toma-hawk at him as if by accident, narrowly missing him. Jones threw back the weapon, injured Sharp Shins and again won approval.

Handsome Boy's people captured the border scout, Moses Van Campen, who had earlier injured their chief, Mohawk. Had they known his identity, they would have taken special pleasure in torturing and killing him. Jones learned who he was but, when asked if he knew the prisoner's name, answered truthfully, "I never saw him before." Thus he saved Van Campen's life, for, by the time the wounded Mohawk reached camp, the scout had been taken to the British at Fort Niagara. Mohawk had with him the tomahawk with which Van Campen had struck him and which he had retrieved. Made in France, it had been won by Mohawk in the French-Indian War and, instead of the usual axe, had a knife blade. Its top was hollow to serve as a pipe bowl and its handle bored for a pipe stem. This so fascinated Horatio that he prevailed upon Mohawk to sell it and later handed it down to his descendants, who gave it to William P. Letchworth's Genesee Valley Museum.

On a trip to visit relatives in Canada, Jones's adoptive family halted at Tonawanda Creek because the canoe kept there for crossing the water was on the opposite bank. His offer to swim across and bring it back was met with horrifed protests—witches living in those waters would drown any swimmer. Scorning such superstition, he swam the distance and returned with the canoe whereupon he was received as one come back from the dead, his feat told and re-told until he was seen as a charmed person.

This fame brought him to the attention of a Captain Powell of the British forces at Niagara who offered to buy Horatio's freedom. When his offer was declined, Powell told Great Hunter he could name any price, as the British king had unlimited funds. "The Great Spirit sent this boy to us as a special gift for the good of the Senecas," came the father's reply, "and he cannot be taken from us until the Great Spirit so directs. We have adopted him, and he is considered by all our people one of my own children. Go, tell your master the King, that he is not rich enough to buy Hoc-sa-go-wah. A Seneca will not sell his own blood!" Soon afterward the members of the Hawk clan assembled to elect Horatio a chief with the new name of Ta-ya-da-o-woh-koh meaning "lying across," symbolizing his bonding of whites with Indians.

One of the approximately eighty other white captives of the Senecas was Sarah Whitmore. Twenty years old in the early 1780's, she confided to Horatio her problem that an Indian whom she did not like was urging her to marry him. Her trouble vanished when Horatio asked her to marry him instead. He had previously married an Indian woman by whom he had a son, but she had either died or left him, and the son lived with her clan. Horatio's and Sarah's marriage was solemnized by her accepting from him a gift more valuable than the one her Indian suitor had offered. When the treaty of Fort Stanwix set the pair free at war's end in 1784, they were married in Schenectady by the missionary, the Rev. Samuel Kirkland.

"Handsome Boy" no longer, Horatio was by then a man of twenty-one with adult responsibilities and a difficult decision to make. He said that he had become "as Indian in my tastes and feelings as if I had been born one." Happy as he was living with Indians, he must have felt that he should become independent and take up life in the larger world. Reluctant as his people were to lose him, yet wanting to abide by the treaty, they encouraged him to leave. "Remember that you are one of our children," a chief said, "and whenever you return, a seat shall be given you where your old age may be passed in peace."

The next year Horatio began work as a fur trader. After building log houses in two locations near Seneca Lake, he moved to the intersection of two trails where there was more travel, becoming the first white settler of what would later be Geneva. The couple's son, born in 1786, was named William for Horatio's father and Whitmore for Sarah's family. He was the first white child born on the trail leading west from Utica. Instead of the usual cradle fashioned from a hollow log, his father made him one of boards taken from a wrecked boat. Three more sons were born to the couple before Sarah's death in 1792. (Ironically, two were killed by Indians in 1813.)

One evening soon after Horatio had begun trapping, a man who had lost his way in the forest came to his door for shelter. He was John Jacob Astor, then starting his career as a trader. Buying Horatio's entire stock of furs on the spot, he hired him to collect pelts exclusively for him and to deliver them to New York City; theirs was a relationship which continued many years. Joseph Smith, a former white captive, moved near the Joneses and was employed by Horatio for a while.

In 1788 Jones began his nearly forty years' service as an interpreter for the United States Government. Appointed by George Washington, he first translated negotiations leading to the Treaty of Buffalo Creek in which the Iroquois sold Nathaniel Gorham and Oliver Phelps all New York State land between the Preemption Line, which ran from Great Sodus Bay along the west bank of Seneca Lake to the Pennsylvania border, and the Genesee plus a tract to the west. Jones traveled to Philadelphia in 1792 with a delegation to the government which included Tall Chief. (Since Tall Chief is said to have dined with Washington, their dinner together may have been during that trip.) The next year Jones helped effect a treaty between the United States and Indians living northwest of the Ohio River. Both he and Jasper Parrish, another former captive turned interpreter, took part in the Big Tree Treaty deliberations in 1797. Here Jones did more than merely interpret: he persuaded the Indians to re-light the council fire when the offended Red Jacket called off negotiations, and he helped Mary Jemison outwit Thomas Morris in obtaining a larger tract of land than Thomas Morris had intended for her.

Meanwhile the Jones family had moved to Little Beard's Town (later Cuylerville), where members of Sarah's adoptive family lived. A year after her death, Horatio married Elizabeth Starr, seventeen-year-old daughter of a Cayuga County family, then living at Williamsburg. In 1797 they moved to a farm on 3,000 acres between Geneseo and Little Beard's Town which was given to them by Indians and which they named Sweet Briar. Their move pleased their Indian friends, who feared that this area was haunted by a headless ghost, but who believed Horatio's magical powers would counteract its evil.

Besides interpreting, Jones carried out various commissions for the government. One assignment, to carry a large sum of government funds to Buffalo Creek, was very dangerous because thieves frequented routes to the Niagara frontier. Jones instructed friends that, if he were killed while in camp, they should look for the money where he would bury it each evening: twenty rods northwest of where he slept. One night on his journey he was awakened by a dream telling him that if he stayed where he was, his bones would be in a pile. Finding no one nearby, he went back to sleep but was again roused by the same dream. Furthermore, something had frightened his horse. Quickly retrieving the money, he rode away and within a few minutes met a man holding a large club but got safely past. Further along the trail he saw a man tending a fire under a large kettle—designed, perhaps, to cook his body into a "pile of bones?" In any event, he reached Buffalo Creek intact.

White settlers credited his influence with preventing Indian raids, and once he did forestall a massacre. Indian warriors had gone to some pioneers' home demanding liquor and, when refused, attacked the family. Jones happened to come upon the scene just in time not only to dissuade the Indians from fighting but also to jolly them into good humor. Lest he be made to sound too saintly, however, there is the anecdote of his meting out pioneer justice to a man known as "the refugee Walker." Walker had the perverse habit of terrorizing settlers with fictitious alarms that Indians were about to attack them. Exasperated by one such tale, Jones struck him with an axe and might have killed him if friends had not interfered. Walker sensibly departed for Canada. Jones's diplomacy no doubt saved the life of Simeon Hovey, a carpenter who had built barns for the Wadsworths and Judge Phelps. In breaking up a fight between two Indians, Hovey hit one with a stick. Other Indians were afraid that the injured man would die and wanted to take "the little carpenter," as they called him, hostage. Jones persuaded them not to with the assurance that, if the man died, Hovey would pay them ten dollars. That satisfied them, besides which, the Indian recovered.

Once an Indian woman was so angry at being excluded from a

pow-wow being held near the Jones home that she set fire to dry hay on the river flatland. Trying to rescue his stock, Jones was surrounded by flames but lay down on a patch of green grass where the wave of fire passed over him. Yet he was not quite invincible. The story is told of a white guide who protested when a crowd of Indians repeatedly threw one of their group into a fire. His interfering in their affairs led the crowd to attack him until Jones appeared and began to fight him alone. It is said that Horatio was then beaten for the first time in his life.

A council of the Six Nations gave Jones and Parrish land near Lake Erie in 1798, when Farmer's Brother said, "They . . . have for several years been serviceable to us as interpreters; we still feel our hearts beat with affection for them and now wish to fulfill the promise we made them for their services."

Horatio Jones must have enjoyed his later years. As a prosperous farmer he associated with the Genesee gentry and still kept contact with old friends. At a dinner given by James Wadsworth to which several Indian chiefs were invited, he and Sharp Shins marked the end of their rivalry by smoking a peace pipe. He saw his and Elizabeth's twelve children become respected citizens. Active throughout his life, he interpreted at the trial of an Indian accused of witch-killing in 1831 and was said to have kept the court and audience in good humor with his remarks.

On one of the annual visits that he and Moses Van Campen exchanged, Jones gave his old friend an awl handle which he had carved from bone and polished with sand during his captivity. He also made a wooden ladle for Van Campen's daughter. J. Niles Hubbard has written of Jones in the 1830's that at this time he was "quite a ubiquitous character; he was here, he was there, and anywhere, and all pretty much at the same time, and more extensively known than any other man in the Genesee country."

Several months before Jones's death in 1836, Charles Augustus Murray met him while visiting James Wadsworth and his daughter, Elizabeth. Murray described the old gentleman as "at heart more than half Indian" and learned from him some Indian lore he used in his story, "The Prairie Bird." Another writer to whom Horatio Jones told Indian legends was William H.C. Hosmer. This man who could not read or write, Hosmer said, "towered in intellectual stature above common men as the pines rise above the smaller trees of the forest."

SOURCES

Harris, George H., "The Life of Horatio Jones"

Hubbard, J. Niles, *Sketches of Border Adventures of Major Moses Van Campen*

Livingston Republican, Apr. 22, 1875

Peer, Sherman, "The Genesee River Historical Sketches"

Turner, Orsamus, *Pioneer History of the Holland Land Purchase*

Micah Brooks, Transplanted New Englander

"I am a schoolteacher from the land of steady habits." With these words Micah Brooks (1775–1857) introduced himself as he walked into the little settlement that was Bloomfield in 1797. To the half-dozen pioneers there, Brooks proposed that he be hired to teach their children. Accepting his offer, they began at once with his help to build a log schoolhouse.

This young man's self-assurance must have impressed the settlers, for his academic credentials could not have. He had had less than twelve months' formal education. A contemporary writer said of him, "The small library of his father, a good native intellect, intercourse with the world, a laudable ambition and self-reliance supplied the rest." If asked his qualifications, Micah probably would have replied merely that he was a New Englander.

Born in 1775 in Cheshire, Connecticut, he was the son of a minister who, after graduating from Yale, had fought in the Revolution and served in the state legislature. His mother was descended from some of the first New Haven colonists. Young Micah typified the pioneer Yorker. Like many others, he was a product of the New England respect for learning and integrity. Transplanted to New York, the inheritors of this tradition were infused with new energy and forward-looking ideas.

A report by one of Schoolmaster Brooks's pupils gives an example of his progressiveness:

> In this school most of us learned for the first time that the earth was round ... I shall never forget the teacher's manner of illustrating these facts: For the want of a globe, he took an old hat, ... marked with a chalk a line round the middle for the equator and another for the eliptic and ... turning it commenced the two revolutions. The simultaneous shout which went up

from small to great was a 'caution' to all young schoolmasters how they introduce new things to young Pioneers. Although the schoolmaster was a favorite with parents and pupils, the most orthodox thought he was talking of something of which he knew nothing . . . , for everybody knew that the earth was flat and immovably fixed, and that the sun rose and set every day.

The protests of the "most orthodox" could not have availed, for Brooks returned to Bloomfield following a summer at home where he learned surveying from a Yale professor. After that second year's teaching (when he added surveying to the curriculum), Micah walked the Niagara Trail to the Falls and thence to Fort Erie in Canada. He later wrote that seeing Lake Erie made him reflect that "the goodness of a Supreme Being has prepared a new creation, ready to be occupied by the people of His choice." He wondered, "At what point will the shores of this beautiful lake be adorned with dwellings and all the appointments of civilized life, as now seen upon the shores of the Atlantic?"

By doing chores for the settler with whom he boarded and hiring out as a hand during haying and harvesting, Brooks saved enough to buy farmland, even though the year 1799 chanced to be one of inflation with land at the high cost of six dollars an acre. The next year he transported building materials from Connecticut to Bloomfield and built a small framed house. He was then commissioned to lay out a road from Canandaigua to Olean as well as one from Hornellsville to the mouth of the Genesee. A year later he brought his two sisters west, to be followed another year by his bride, Mary Hall of Lyme, Connecticut.

From then on, this man's career advanced from one distinguished position to another. A member of the State militia, he fought in the War of 1812 and eventually rose to the rank of major general. First appointed justice of the peace, he was later made assistant justice of the Ontario County courts and then sent to the State Assembly from the county. As early as 1810, even before Gov. DeWitt Clinton advocated it, he urged the construction of a canal and became one of the moving forces in the Erie Canal project. He also served as a State loan commissioner lending money to farmers.

In 1814 Micah Brooks was elected to Congress to represent all of New York State west of Cayuga Lake. One of his acts was to procure government mail service through Rochester. He initiated a bill whereby the national government would help finance the Erie Canal. It passed both houses, but was vetoed by President Madison, making Brooks a staunch opponent of the executive veto power.

His surveying work had acquainted Brooks with the land which the Senecas had held out from Robert Morris and given to Mary Jemison in 1797. He and two associates had long wanted to buy land from her, but could not because, as a ward of the government, she was not a United States citizen. Congressman Brooks introduced legislation making Mary a citizen. When it passed in 1823, he hastened to the Gardeau Flats to congratulate her on her elevated status and (shrewdly enough) bought from her at fifty cents an acre six thousand acres.

Now the father of seven children, Brooks built a home on the Transit Line Road between Nunda and Mt. Morris. There he established over the years the community of Brooks Grove. He was appointed its postmaster by Gideon Granger of Canandaigua, Postmaster-General in Jefferson's administration. Besides his home, barn and carriage house, it included a church and school for which he gave the land, other residences and a hotel. He remarried after his first wife's death and fathered three more children.

During the 1830's, Brooks supported the construction of the Genesee Valley Canal and the enlarging of the Erie Canal. A speech he delivered at a convention of railroad men led to the building of the Erie Railway. As a charter member of the Livingston County Agricultural Society, he helped draft its constitution in 1841. Meanwhile, he added twelve thousand more acres to his land holdings. Once while riding in Allegany County timberland, he met a man cutting shingles and asked him if he owned the trees. "No," he was told, "they belong to Old Man Brooks, but he owns so much land he doesn't know what's going on."

Micah Brooks lived to enjoy the respect of many for his industry, intelligence and public spirit. In the fullness of eighty-two years, he died suddenly in 1857.

This patriarch had once written a letter to a local paper in tribute to the first settlers of the region. "Under the energy, industry, perserverance and economy of that class of Puritans," he wrote, "they subdued the forests, built the schoolhouses and the churches ... and, with the family use of their public libraries produced some of the brightest ornaments of society in science and literature and the ablest of our statesmen." He himself was one of that number.

SOURCES

Brooks, Merle W., Personal interview
Turner, Orsamus, *History of the Pioneer Settlement of Phelps and Gorham's Purchase*

General Micah Brooks

Gen. William Mills, "Big Kettle"

The Mills Mansion, restored by the Mt. Morris Historical Society, is the home of General William A. Mills (1777–1844), that town's first permanent white settler. It is the fourth home that Mills built, and the progression of the four from rusticity to elegance tells a pioneer's success story.

William was the son of Samuel Mills, a Presbyterian missionary of Williamsburg, New York, the colony established by Col. Charles Williamson. Samuel preached in the open air, in people's homes and in a Williamsburg warehouse until he died of the so-called "Genesee fever," or malaria, in 1794. Though the rest of the family returned to Connecticut, William, aged seventeen, chose to stay in the Valley. He first rented, then later bought land on the flats, hiring Indians to farm it. One day his horse slipped between the logs forming the road and broke a leg, which cost the young man most of his first summer's profit.

Mills built his first house, a log cabin, at Allan's Hill where the mansion now stands. There he lived alone, or, as the historian, Lockwood L. Doty, phrased it, "kept bachelor hall."

In 1800 he built the village's first block house on Stanley Street. Its walls were of timber flattened on both sides and its roof of staves split from oak logs. Three years later he built a substantial log house to which he brought his bride. She was Susannah Harris, who had come from Pennsylvania on horseback along an Indian trail to visit her brother in Williamsburg. As Mills's daughter later told the story, he visited Harris—ostensibly, at least—to borrow a hoe, and the couple were soon engaged to marry. As there was no mail service between the Valley and northern Pennsylvania, they decided before she returned home that their wedding would take place exactly one year from the day they parted. He spent the time building his third home, while she spun and wove to make enough clothes and bedding to last for several years. She brought with her the first mirror in Mt. Morris.

Soon after sunrise on the day William was to arrive in Pennsylvania for the wedding, Susannah walked outdoors and saw him riding up on a shiny black horse. One historian has recorded that the couple made additions to their house "as required." Since they raised ten children in it, it must have expanded.

Finally in 1838 Mills built the mansion, a federal-style structure of locally-made bricks. It is distinguished by a handsome walnut staircase cantilevered along a curved wall.

Fluent in the Seneca language, Mills was a friend of Tall Chief and Red Jacket. He rented land on Gardeau Flats from Mary Jemison, who stopped at his home to bid him good-bye when she left the Valley. The Indians named him Sa-nen-ga-wa, or Big Kettle, meaning "generous man." He never let a person who bought land from him lose it for lack of payment. In 1816, the "year without a summer," when frost destroyed the crops in Allegany County, a delegation came to Mills asking for wheat and corn with the promise of paying later. He filled their sleighs with corn, grain and pork, and at the next harvest they came back to repay him in full with their labor.

Mills helped organize Mt. Morris as a town, served as its first justice of the peace and was a supervisor for twenty years. He also contributed to building its first church and helped secure its first dam. Active in the organization of Livingston County, he was also a director of its first bank, founder of its Agricultural Society and member of a committee which brought a railroad to the Valley.

After fighting in the War of 1812, William Mills organized the county's first military company and became a major general in the State militia with command over six counties. (It was at this time, incidentally, that the Indians called Mrs. Mills "Captain.") In a letter written for the Mt. Morris centennial celebration in 1894, Mrs. Eunice Hall recalled the companies' training sessions on the village green. She described their sham battles, bugle calls and martial music, saying that their "boom of cannon and rattle of musketry resounded the hills around." She remembered General Mills riding an old war horse of General Winfield Scott's, which was "prancing and curvetting as if he bore the old brigadier again on the field of battle."

"Oh, the splendor of General Mills," she exclaimed, "with his military cocked hat and waving plumes and gold-laced regimentals, with glittering epauletts, long flowing crimson silken scarf and the flashing sword and scabbard at his side. When he waved the bright blade in his gauntleted hand, giving orders as he reviewed the fine platoon of glittering bayonettes, he looked every inch a hero."

SOURCES

Doty, Lockwood L., *History of Livingston County*

Parsons, Levi and Rockfellow, Samuel L, eds., *Centennial Celebration, Mt. Morris, N. Y.*

Smith, James H., *History of Livingston County, N. Y.*

Turner, Orsamus, *History of the Pioneer Settlement of Phelps and Gorham's Purchase*

Mt. Morris

The Versatile Philip Church

Having come in the mid-1770's from England to America where he associated with the socially elite, John Barker Church had every reason to side with the Tories. Yet he had emigrated for the express purpose of aiding the American Revolution and served as commissary officer to the French forces in the war. He formed friendships with such patriots as Alexander Hamilton and Gen. Philip Schuyler, marrying the General's daughter, Angelica.

The couple's son, Philip (1778–1861), was an equally staunch American patriot. A scar on his forehead which he bore through life may have been a constant reminder of his alienation from Britain. When he was a baby, his mother had taken him to visit her parents in Albany. Suddenly one day a group of Tories and Indians tried to capture General Schuyler. They forced the members of the household to the second story where Philip's aunt, realizing that he had been left downstairs, ran to his rescue. An Indian threw a tomahawk at them, grazing the baby's forehead. The family was saved by a clever trick of the General's. He called out the window (to no one), "My friends, my friends, quickly surround the house and let not one of the rascals escape!" This set "the rascals" running.

After the war the Churches lived in Paris where they resumed acquaintance with Lafayette. Later, while living in London, they entertained such notables as Fox and Pitt, as well as refugees from the French Revolution including Tallyrand. Philip's loyalty to America cost him dearly when he attended Eton, for his classmates, resenting England's loss of her colonies, teased him as only schoolboys can. He went on to study law at London's Middle Temple.

Returning to America in 1797, Philip continued his studies with a New York City attorney. He also served as secretary to

Alexander Hamilton, the husband of his mother's sister. This work often included carrying messages to General Washington, and on those occasions Hamilton usually advised his nephew to impress the Genral by being punctual. When Philip applied for an Army commission, Washington at first thought him too young, but recalling his habit of punctuality made him a captain.

In the last year of the old century, this young gentleman stood on the the verge of a career which promised the enjoyment of culture, refinement and material comforts, but he made a trip that radically changed his life. He went as his father's agent to Canandaigua to buy 100,000 acres of land in what later became Allegany County. John Church offered him a half interest in the property in exchange for his subdividing and selling it. On his return to New York City, Philip and his father visited a gentlemen's club. As they were conversing with a group of distinguished men, the talk turned to the bad condition of the road between New York and Albany. Philip asserted that there would be a good turnpike road between Albany and Canandaigua before there was one along the Hudson. All his elders pronounced him "beside himself," and his father afterward rebuked him for his foolishness, but Philip's prediction proved generally correct.

Admitted to the bar in 1804, Philip Church practiced law for only a few months. The task of subdividing his family's Genesee Valley land called him to a totally different life. With a party of four he traveled to Bath. There he met Col. Charles Williamson, who recommended as a surveyor Maj. Moses Van Campen, whereupon Church set out for Almond to find him. The Van Campen family first saw him as a stranger in their cornfield vigorously shaking out his clothes. About an hour later when Church appeared and introduced himself, they learned that he had been getting rid of fleas he had picked up in the woods.

A firm friendship began as Van Campen led Church on his first exploration of southwestern New York's forests. Withstanding almost constant rain, the group traveled across the tract, learning its rivers, hills and valleys in order to divide it wisely. Philip is said to have climbed the tallest pines on the highest hills of a certain area to choose the site of his property's first village. Naming it Angelica for his mother, he opened a land-sales office and designated the lots around a future central square as the sites for four churches.

Continuing their hike, Church and Van Campen reached the northwest portion of the tract. There they decided to cap off their journey with a little excursion to see Niagara Falls. Several days' walk took them to Buffalo, as the historian, Orsamus Turner, described them "with torn clothes, beards unshaven, tanned and camp-smoked." From the Falls they stopped at the newly-established Batavia land office, then called on the Wadsworths in Geneseo.

In the next several years Church supervised the running of a store and the building of a saw mill, a grist mill and a road to Angelica from the outskirts of Hornellsville. In 1804 he built a home called "the White House," since for some years it was the only painted house west of Canandaigua. The next year he took to it his bride, the former Anna Matilda Stewart, beautiful daughter of Gen. Walter Stewart of Philadelphia, a close friend of Washington. The pair traveled via stagecoach to Bath, in a wagon to Hornellsville and by horseback along a marked trail to Angelica. Anna Church later spoke lightly of having adapted as an eighteen-year-old socialite to pioneer life, saying, "I was just the one to do it. I had youth and health. To be sure, it was pretty hard at first, but the relations of a wife, to which was added the cares of a mother, soon reconciled me to my new home."

Church began the building of his permanent home, Belvidere, in 1807. Situated amid a 2000-acre tract about four miles outside Angelica, it stood on a hill overlooking the Genesee with a wide view of the valley framed by gradually rising hills. Its architect was Benjamin Latrobe, who designed the national Capitol for President Jefferson. Built in the Greek Revival style, the mansion had a spacious porch with stately Ionic columns made from pine trees. It was made of stone quarried from a neighboring creek and of bricks made in the area. Costing $9800, Belvidere had walls two feet thick, large rooms and thirteen fireplaces. One room was used as a land office, replacing the log building in the village. Because of a shortage of skilled workers, it took five years to complete the mansion, though the family moved into it in 1810. Mrs. Church supervised the planting of trees, shrubs and a formal garden and left standing many first-growth oaks. On the property was a grove of oaks and elms where the Indians of Caneadea camped when hunting in the vicinity.

The historian, John Minard, has said of Anna Church that

"her kindness to the poor was such as to excite comment." She often attended the Indians' feasts and dances at Caneadea, bringing gifts of food. The Senecas adopted her into a tribe and gave her a name meaning "the first white woman who has come." Philip Church was visiting in England when the War of 1812 broke out, preventing his return home. Thus when the Caneadea Indians heard gunfire at Fort Erie, they offered to place a guard around Belvidere to protect Mrs. Church from attack by pro-British Indians of Canada. Valley lore has given this story alternative endings. One states that Mrs. Church believed she was in no danger and declined her friends' offer of help with thanks. The other holds that, when her husband returned home, she told him that she had been frightened by Indians who had gathered at the gate, to which he replied, "Nonsense! I stationed them there to take care of you. Those were *my* Indians!"

During his enforced stay in England, Church studied that country's latest farming methods. After his return home he used this knowledge to benefit his area by importing five breeds of sheep and cattle. A judge of the County Court of Common Pleas, he was an incorporator of the Lake Erie Turnpike Company and one of the first to support the building of the Genesee Valley Canal. He had the foresight, however, to think that it would be wiser to build a railroad than a canal and he did that also as a leading backer of the New York and Erie Railroad.

After their first years on the frontier, the Churches lived very comfortably. They had a large library, hired a tutor for their nine children and often entertained visitors, among them Gov. DeWitt Clinton and Horatio Seymour. Mrs. Church's parents came from Philadelphia in a coach and four to visit, and the John B. Churches several times brought up a party from New York City. In the mood of Marie Antoinette at a picnic, they traveled with a wagonload of provisions, including formal dinner service. As they camped in the wilderness, they dined on freshly caught fish and game roasted over an open fire by their French chef. He had once cooked for the King of England, but his opinions in favor of the French Republic had made him so unwelcome in the royal kitchen that it was arranged for the senior Mr. Church to bring him to America's democratic shores. His son, Louis Godey, became the founder of the popular magazine, "Godey's Lady's Book."

The Philip Church family attended a reception in Rochester

for General Lafayette during his 1824 tour of America. As one of the daughters was about to be introduced, the General interposed, "Sir, you need not introduce this young lady, she is a descendant of my old friend, Angelica Schuyler."

Besides his other advantages, Philip Church enjoyed good health throughout his long life. Always athletic, he outraced the fastest Indian runners several times and played cricket well into old age. His expert marksmanship was shown in a match with Van Campen when the target was a small bit of paper stuck onto a tree with a pin. One of the two not only hit the paper, but drove the pin into the tree trunk. When the other made his shot, no second hole was found, causing some onlookers to claim he had missed the tree entirely. But someone chopped into the tree and found both balls in the same hole.

Church enjoyed life at Belvidere until his death at age eighty-three. It is probable that he still had the love for his home that he had once expressed in a letter written from England, "Although I am delighted with the beauties of England, my visit has a contrary effect from what I expected; it has increased my attachment to Angelica."

SOURCES

Hubbard, J. Niles, *Sketches of the Life of Moses VanCampen*
McNall, Neil, "The Landed Gentry of the Genesee"
Minard, John S., *The Story of John Barker Church*
Thornton, Winifred K., "A History of the Church Mansion, Belvidere"

Public Buildings, Angelica

A Tree, Two Men, A Village and A Treaty

The phrase, "Big Tree," has four references, all interesting. Probably the earliest is to the actual tree, a giant white oak. Though not remarkable for its height—an estimated seventy feet—it was twenty-eight feet in circumference. The Indians revered it and had a compact with the first settlers that it would never be injured by axe or fire. It stood on land owned by James and William Wadsworth in present-day Geneseo on the east bank of the Genesee.

The Big Tree lived long past its prime. It would have survived even longer if the river had not changed its course and undermined it. In its last years, an elm tree grew up from under its roots, entwining itself through the old tree's branches and depriving it of nourishment. An unknown local writer saw this as symbolizing the white man's defeat of the Indian:

> Crushed in the Saxon's treacherous grasp
> The Indian's heart is broke—
> The graceful Elm's insidious clasp
> Destroys the mighty Oak!

In the twentieth century, on the other hand, this image has suggested new life from old roots.

Although General James S. Wadsworth, son and nephew of the pioneers, tried for years to prop up the veteran tree with rocks and brush, the flooding river finally toppled it in 1857. Wadsworth had it cut in sections and drawn by a team of oxen to his home. His son later gave a section to William P. Letchworth, who placed it under a rustic summer house. Another section was moved to the grounds of the Livingston County Historical Society museum.

Secondly, "Big Tree' is the equivalent of Go-on-dah-go-wah,

the name of the Seneca chief who farmed land surrounding the tree. The brother of Mary Jemison's adoptive mother, he took part in the Treaty of Buffalo Creek at which Oliver Phelps and Nathaniel Gorham bought their land in 1788. The author Lydia Sigourney has recorded that when William Wadsworth paraded a company of fifty or sixty men (collected from many miles around) before his and his brother's log house in 1780, Chief Go-on-dah-go-wah came to watch. James Wadsworth noticed that he looked very sad and asked him the reason. Pointing first to the soldiers, then to the few Indians standing by, Big Tree answered, "You are the rising sun; but we are the setting sun." Covering his head with his blanket, he wept.

This chief's daughter married a Niagara trader, Pollard, and their son bore the slightly different name, Go-on-do-wau-nah, also meaning Big Tree. His other title was Col. John Pollard. He fought in border wars and at the Wyoming, Pennsylvania, massacre. He has been ranked as an orator second only to Red Jakcet and compared to Cornplanter in integrity. One of the first Indians on the Buffalo Creek reservation to become a Christian, he died there in 1841.

A third use of "Big Tree" is as the name of both a settlement and the land surrounding it. The former was the few structures in the southwest corner of the present Village of Geneseo, the latter the 2,000 acres which the Wadsworth brothers had bought from their uncle, Jeremiah Wadsworth. A number of early sources refer to this community as "Big Tree." Further evidence that this was Geneseo's original name is the fact that several streets in other towns which lead to Geneseo have that name.

Finally there is the Treaty of the Big Tree of 1797. According to Horatio Jones, who was present, the treaty was named for the village, rather than for the tree. Thomas Morris acting for his father Robert, who called the council, built a large house roofed with boughs and branches for the negotiations. It was near a log house of the Wadsworths, which he rented so that he could entertain the council's leading participants.

Robert Morris' purpose in initiating the meeting was to buy all the Senecas' land west of the Genesee River. He had already bought this property from the Commonwealth of Massachusetts, to which it then belonged, but had never cleared his title to it by paying the Indians for it. By 1797 he was in the difficult position of being forced to buy it because he had already sold it out from under the Indians' feet to some buyers in Holland, who were holding back part of the purchase price until he should extinguish the Indians' title to it.

Besides Thomas Morris, the white men participating included Jeremiah Wadsworth as commissioner representing the United States Government, several other officials plus Horatio Jones and Jasper Parrish as interpreters. Among the fifty-two Indians present were Handsome Lake, Red Jacket, Cornplanter, Little Beard, Destroy Town and the second Big Tree.

Negotiations did not proceed smoothly. Red Jacket opposed the sale and at one point declared the council closed. Desperate to resume it, Morris gave presents to all the women. He knew that the land actually belonged to the warriors who defended it and the women who tilled it. Thus the women could and did re-open the council.

Morris' offer of $100,000 was disputed. Since the Indians had no idea of how much that was, it had to be explained how many casks of a certain size would be needed to hold that amount and how many horses to pull it. The Government required that the purchase money be invested in United States Bank stock and held in trust for the Seneca nation. With no knowledge of investment theory, the Indians thought that a bank was a field in Philadelphia where money was planted, producing better crops in some years than in others. Later they often asked Morris what kind of crop they could expect that season.

There was also difficulty in determining the boundaries of ten reservations which the Indians held back from sale. They wanted them described in terms of natural features, such as the course of a stream, but the whites would not give them that advantage and insisted on the use of arbitrary measurements. Since the Indians did not know the difference, for example, between a square mile and a mile square, they were cheated. The one exception to this was Mary Jemison's acquiring the Gardeau reservation. Claiming that she had improved her land in various spots, she named certain boundaries which Morris wrongly assumed comprised only about 150 acres and thus obtained nearly 18,000 acres of fertile bottomland. She was the one person the white men did not cheat.

One reason the Indians lost so much was that they expected the settlers to use the land as they, themselves, had. They saw themselves not so much owning the land as being custodians of it. They did not rob or exploit the soil, but took from it only what they needed. Of course the pioneers thought them a primitive people.

SOURCES

"American Historical Trees," *Harper's New Monthly Magazine*
Doty, Lockwood R., *History of Livingston County*
Samson, William H., "The Treaty of Big Tree"
Sigourney, Mrs. L. H., *Scenes In My Native Land*
Wadsworth, Elizabeth, Letter to Mrs. Sigourney

Village of Geneseo

Elisha Johnson, Imaginative Engineer

Rochester is indebted to Elisha Johnson (c.1784–1866) for many contributions, all constructive and useful. His portrait shows him as a most dignified gentleman with an expression so severe that it is almost fierce. Yet he built one thing, Hornby Lodge at Portage, which shows his hidden romantic nature.

After attending Williams College, Johnson began his career in 1807 surveying and subdividing 3,000 acres of the Cotringer tract, which consisted of 50,000 acres surrounding Portage in what are now Wyoming and Livingston Counties.

He moved to Rochesterville in 1817, the year it was incorporated into a village, and with Orson Seymour paid $10,000 for eighty acres, much of it still forested. This he surveyed and laid out as part of the village. Meanwhile he built a dam across the river near where the Erie Railroad later stood. Also in that year he and his partner constructed the Johnson-Seymour raceway, or canal, from the east end of his dam to the Main Street bridge. This gave other settlers the opportunity to establish flour and paper mills.

Three years later Johnson gave New York State land from the east bank to the middle of the Genesee for an aqueduct to carry water across the river as part of the Erie Canal; three years after that he built the city's first horse-drawn railroad, which ran three miles from the south end of Water Street to Carthage. He followed this enterprise by becoming surveyor, contractor and chief engineer of the Tonawanda Railroad, which first extended out of Rochester to South Byron and then later as far as Attica. The train ran on Johnson's invention of tracks made by fastening flat iron bars onto stringers laid on heavy blocks of wood set endwise into the ground. He received a patent signed by President Andrew Jackson for this in 1835.

Nor were engineering works his only gift to Rochester. Beginning in 1827, he was elected president of Rochesterville Village for three terms. An organizer and member of the first vestry of St. Paul's Episcopal Church, he was also a trustee of the Franklin Institute, a society formed to promote literary and scientific pursuits. In 1838 he was chosen the fifth mayor of what was by then known as the city of Rochester. In the hope that it would be the site of a city hall, he gave the land called Washington Square. Naming St. Paul Street after the church, he suggested the name, Mt. Hope, for a new cemetery as well.

Engineering claimed his efforts again when from 1840 to 1842 he directed the digging of a tunnel as part of the Genesee Valley Canal. This entailed the stupendous feat of digging into the palisades at Portage, which, except for the use of dynamite, was done entirely by hand.

It was then that Elisha Johnson departed from his serviceable and prosaic assignments to build what may have been the most fanciful home ever seen in the Valley. Wanting to be near his work and to have his family with him, he positioned the house directly over the future tunnel site. At this time various individualists throughout the northeast were building octagonal houses. Later, in 1856, when Orson Fowler wrote a book showing that they enclosed more space and enjoyed more sunlight and ventilation than conventional houses, they became quite popular. In Hornby Lodge, which he named for the original white owners of the land, Johnson not only anticipated this fad—he out-did it.

Although his house was called an octagon, it actually had sixteen sides. A true octagon house has the four corners of a square cut away with walls built across the openings. His house had the corners cut away and square rooms set diagonally onto the openings. A large center room called the grand saloon, thirty-two feet square, opened on its four long sides onto verandas and on its four cut-away sides onto a parlor, library, office and kitchen. Four stories high, the structure had eighteen rooms. The upper stories were square, their corners projecting over the wings below. The top floor, called an observatory, featured windows in the roof which gave onto a spectacular view of the Middle and Upper Falls in one direction and the Lower Falls in another.

The Gothic, or picturesque, motif was carried into the interior. The trunk of a white oak tree three feet in diameter, its bark left on and its roots showing, supported the ceiling of the grand saloon. A stairway cut into the tree wound up to the observatory. Probably inspired by William Henry Harrison's presidential campaign of 1840, which featured log cabins, this room was made entirely of logs with bark still on. Its furniture, consisting chiefly of couches, was made from branches and the floor covered with natural-toned matting. A cabinet around the base of the central tree trunk displayed local geological specimens. In every corner sat stuffed squirrels, racoons and chipmunks, and stuffed birds perched on crooked branches. The grounds, Tunnel Park, were kept uncultivated.

The noted painter Thomas Cole, made a drawing of Hornby Lodge when he was a guest there, and a Johnson daughter had her wedding in it. Such a curiosity attracted almost as many visitors as the Falls themselves. This came to an end, however, when excavating for the tunnel beneath the house was abandoned, and blasting for a substitute route around the cliff made it unsafe to live in. When it was torn down in 1849, the Valley lost what had been the imaginative work of an otherwise practical man.

SOURCES

McKelvey, Blake, *Rochester the Water Power City 1812-1854*
Parker, Jane M., *Rochester: A Story Historical*
Peck, William F., "Elisha Johnson"

Hornby Lodge

John Crawford In "The Land of the Free"

The day's work had been hard, and, though the sun was setting, the heat in the Virginia field was still ferocious. If his former master had lived, John thought, he would have let the hands quit work at sundown. His old master had been good to him, trusting him with special errands, even letting him take the plantation's produce to market in Richmond, Petersburg and Norfolk.

But the overseer that the mistress had recently hired showed the men no mercy. He had just told them to hang up their scythes and start to bind and shock the rye they had cut all day. Tired and hungry as they were, the others obeyed, but John hung onto his scythe. It was as if he had known this moment would come.

The overseer walked toward him, whip in hand. "You're not going to do as you're told?" he growled.

Almost to his surprise, John heard himself say he would do no more work that day. Furious, the white man dashed toward the slave, his whip raised to strike. "Keep your distance," John said quietly, "or I'll cut you down with this scythe. I won't be whipped!"

The overseer came no closer and called on the men to help. But they knew John's strength as well as his determination and did not move. The overseer said he would settle with John later and started the others on their night's work.

Going to his hut, John told his wife to bring him his supper outdoors, as he would not be caged inside. All that night and the next day, a Sunday, he hid in a place where he could see all that passed around the main house but could not be seen. On Monday morning John saw two overseers from neighboring plantations ride up to the house. With them were three bloodhounds. When he saw his overseer greet the others, John knew it was time to act.

He came out into the open field within hearing distance of the men. His overseer called to him to come to the house. "No," John said, "Unless you promise not to whip me."

"I'll do no such thing. You come here and then we'll see what your punishment will be."

"I won't be whipped!"

"We'll set the dogs on you if you don't come here!"

"I'm ready for them." And the dogs were let loose and told to seize him.

John waited quietly until they were at a full run and almost upon him, when suddenly he turned about and commanded the dogs in a loud, confident voice, "Seize him!" and ran ahead of them toward the woods about a mile away.

Completely misled, the dogs streaked past their quarry in full chase of some unknown victim. John followed, cheering them on in their pursuit, until he reached the woods. From that cover he could see three men vainly trying to catch up to him. By now he was safe, as the dogs and he were the best of friends. They kept up their hunt for a runaway, and John hid himself.

The story of his escape was told by John Crawford (1789–1864) to a man known today only as "M," an old resident of Geneseo, who recounted it in a letter to the *Livingston Republican* when the former slave died at age seventy-five in 1864. John's last name actually was one he chose himself, and he never revealed his former master's name or where he lived more than to say it was near Richmond.

John's troubles were far from over on that first day of freedom, as "M's" re-telling describes. That evening he met his wife, who gave him a bundle of food and clothes. He told her he was going North and would come back for her someday. Guided by the North Star, he traveled for many nights, hiding during the day. Except for the time he found some half-grown potatoes, he suffered severely from hunger.

After many weary miles, guessing that he was in a free state, he went to a house to beg bread. The woman of the household, sensing he was a runaway, told him that he should go to Philadelphia, where he would find friends. There he was helped to make his way to Canada where he found work and saved some money. After several years he took the risk of returning to his old home to free his wife but learned that soon after his escape she had been sold "down in Dixie." Again he made his way North, this time reaching Geneseo.

At first he worked for one H. Spencer and other farmers. Later, his obituary states, "He for many years acted as the village deliveryman and with his wheelbarrow labeled 'Crawford's Express' was to be seen at all hours of the day around the village streets with a pleasant smile on his face and a kind word for all he met." He was a member of the Methodist Church and for a long time its sexton.

"He was possessed of a strong mind and intelligence and goodness of heart that made him respected by all," the obituary continues. "The rich and the poor, the high and the low all recognized 'old John,' and there is hardly a family in the village in which he will not be missed. He was of a strong religious turn of mind and, after escaping to the land of the free, learned to read, and he was conversant with the Bible from beginning to end. He lived a good and true man and died in the faith of a blessed future . . ."

"M" ended his letter with these words, "We shall all miss him, for he had grown into a village necessity. Reports say he salted away a good many sixpences in the good old days when silver coin was in vogue. Peace to his remains. We shall not soon forget him. He was a very sensible, shrewd man and abhorred slavery with all his might."

SOURCE

Livingston Republican, Jan. 28, 1864

Charles Finney, Lighter of Fires

"I was not a little irritable," Charles Finney (1792–1875) later confessed in his memoirs. A young lawyer recently arrived in Adams, New York, from New Jersey in 1819, he had joined a prayer group and was asked if he wanted the other members to pray for him. He declined, saying that, though he was indeed a sinner in need of prayers, theirs would do no good. "You have been praying for a revival of religion ever since I have been in Adams, and yet you have it not," he told them. "You have prayed enough since I have attended these meetings to have prayed the devil out of Adams if there is any virtue in your prayers. But here you are, praying on and complaining still!" History does not record his friends' reaction to Finney's outburst, but it does accord him the place of nineteenth-century America's outstanding revivalist.

Tall, athletic and handsome, Finney was a sociable and popular man whose only acquaintance with the Bible had been to study Mosaic law during his legal training. He rejected the preaching he had heard, which held that humans are utterly and hopelessly sinful. Beginning to study the Bible on his own, he decided why his friends' petitions went unanswered. It was because they did not follow the Bible's requirement to pray with complete certainty that God would give them what they asked for. As he attempted to find God, he became painfully aware of his own self-centeredness. Much soul-searching led him to believe that nothing more than his own willed consent was needed for salvation, and with this conviction he was converted to Christianity. Some highly emotional experiences then assured him that salvation was offered not only to the elect, but to all. He then felt compelled to devote his life to preaching the gospel. After a five-year study of theology, he was ordained a Presbyterian minister in 1824.

Church-going Americans were then in the throes of what is

called the Second Great Awakening, the first having taken place in the 1730's and 1740's. A renewed interest in religion had led hundreds of young men to enter the ministry. Moving toward the frontier, which in the North was then Western New York, they conducted scores of revivals. That area was called the "Burned-over District," implying that the many revivals which had swept over it like wildfire had left but few persons to be converted.

Charles Finney came onto this stage ideally suited for his mission. His attractive personality, powerful delivery, informal manners and independent spirit fitted him to revivalism as a hand to its glove. Revivals aim to persuade people of their sinfulness in order to impel them to seek forgiveness. Finney discarded the then-orthodox belief in moral depravity and assured people that they could repent and find faith. He threatened sinners with the terrors of hell-fire, but promised salvation to all who chose it.

Finney conducted revivals throughout Western New York as well as in New York City and Pennsylvania with spectacular results. He spoke in every-day language, often praying for sinners by name, persuading, brow-beating, somehow forcing them into repentance. His preaching often caused people to faint, shriek, weep, even fall into seizures. He was criticized for this by other clergymen, but he believed that people would not act unless they were excited and refused to change a method which brought in so many converts. "Better a full church with undignified preaching than an empty one with it," he said.

In 1831 Charles Finney was invited to preach at Rochester's Third Presbyterian Church where he stayed six months. He left a city quite different from the one he had found. As he first saw it, Rochester was "full of thrift and enterprise and full of sin." Later he could write, "The change in the order, sobriety and morality of the city was wonderful." Preaching many times a week to audiences of all denominations, the evangelist doubled the city's church membership. He caused taverns to be closed, a theater turned into a livery stable and high school classes suspended for prayer. Divisions within churches and between denominations were healed. The scholar, Whitney Cross, has stated that no more impressive revival has occurred in America history.

For Rochesterians Finney moderated his former excesses, adopting a serious, dignified manner and presenting his case for Christ with lawyer-like logic. He admittedly directed his message first to community leaders knowing that others would follow their example. His preaching was so powerful that, for instance, when he pointed to the ceiling and dropped his hand to describe a sinner's fall into hell, people in the rear seats stood up to see the descent.

During this revival Finney began his custom of seating people who wanted to be converted on an "anxious bench"—from which they predictably fell. Prayer meetings, some lasting all night, were held throughout the six months; laypersons were trained to counsel converts; and volunteers canvassed the city door-to-door. The influence of this revival spread beyond Rochester to other revivals held as far away as New England and Ohio—all inspired by this man who claimed, "If Christians united and dedicated their lives to the task, they could convert the world and bring on the millennium in three months."

Finney returned to Rochester to conduct revivals in 1842 and 1855–1856. The city's high opinion of him was reciprocated, for he wrote:

> I have never preached anywhere with more pleasure than in Rochester. The people . . . have manifested a candor, an earnestness and an appreciation of the truth excelling anything I have seen on so large a scale in any other place. I have labored in other cities where the people were even more highly educated than in Rochester. But in those cities the views and habits of the people were more stereotyped; the people were more fastidious, more afraid of measures than in Rochester.

Lyman Beecher, an evangelist who had previously criticized Finney for undue emotionalism, later said of his first Rochester crusade that 100,000 persons throughout the country joined churches in 1831 as a result of "the greatest revival of religion the world has ever seen." More temperate praise comes from historians who consider his work a force leading to the many reform movements of mid-nineteenth-century America.

SOURCES

Cross, Whitney, *The Burned-over District*
Eisenburger, Bernard, *They Gathered at the River*
"Finney, Charles Grandison" *Dictionary of American Biography*
Johnson, Paul E., *A Shopkeeper's Millennium: Society and Revivals in Rochester*
McLoughlin, William G., *Modern Revivals*

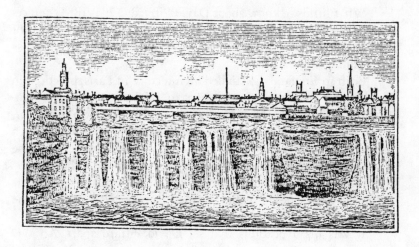

Genesee Falls at Rochester

David Piffard, Cultured Pioneer

What little we know about David Piffard (1794–1883) depicts an accomplished and humanitarian gentleman. The village of Piffard, part of the town of York, was originally named for him as Piffardinia.

Born in England, he studied architecture in Paris, practiced in London, then came to this country in 1822 at age twenty-eight. After working with a New York City architectural firm for a year, he arrived in the Genesee Valley. There he bought 600 acres which included Piffardinia as well as the first house built in the area. The next year Piffard returned from a trip to New York with his bride, the former Ann Haight. During the rest of his long life he managed his Genesee Valley farm, together with land that he bought in Pennsylvania and Michigan.

It was his avocations that set David Piffard apart. An avid reader, he was a student of both the arts and sciences. In 1839 he was with Charles Carroll and William Fitzhugh an examiner conducting the Temple Hill Academy public examination in French and Latin, the latter lasting four hours. He had a remarkable memory and was said to be able to talk intelligently on almost any subject. Years before it was generally accepted, he believed the vibratory, or wave-length, theory of light and sound. Usually called Dr. Piffard, he studied medicine entirely on his own and cared for many people in the area, never accepting payment for his services. Perhaps due to this influence, his son Henry became a physician and founded the American Dermatological Association.

The gardens of the Piffards' estate, Oak Forest, were among the Valley's finest showplaces. The couple were noted for their hospitality and their willingness to help any neighbor in need. He was especially fond of children, often taking part in their sports.

Mr. and Mrs. Piffard were at first members of St. Michael's Episcopal Church in Geneseo, he serving on both its first vestry and the building committee for its first structure. As an outgrowth of Mrs. Piffard's teaching a Sabbath school in Piffard, her parents, who visited often, helped the couple establish a Protestant Dutch Reformed Church, which was dedicated in 1846. It later became the First Presbyterian Church, then St. Raphael's Roman Catholic Church and afterward a residence. Piffard also helped establish the Livingston County Agricultural Society.

Mrs. Piffard, an accomplished musician, brought the first piano to the area. The story is told that one day in her husband's absence she was playing and singing by herself. Suddenly she sensed she was not alone. She realized that a group of Indians had silently come into the room and were standing very still, listening. To cover her panic, she kept on playing, bravely managing to sing a little. After what seemed like an eternity, her husband came into the room and crossed over quickly to her. She fainted into his arms. But they say that afterward the Indians, who were friendly, often came to enjoy her music.

SOURCES

"David Piffard," *Biographical Review: The Leading Citizens of Living- and Wyoming Counties, N. Y.*
Livingston Republican, July 5, 1883
Root, Mary, *History of York*

Millard Fillmore's Spectacular Success

Millard Fillmore (1800–1874) lived in the Valley only three months, but during that time he made an important decision: not to let circumstances keep him from getting ahead in the world. Certainly, this "poor but honest" country lad could not have imagined that he would one day be President.

Hard luck struck Fillmore's parents soon after he was born in a proverbial log cabin in Locke, Cayuga County, New York. Since the title to their land was found to be defective, they had to lease another plot, clear it, build another cabin and start over again in Niles, Cayuga County. Millard's schooling was first limited to spelling and reading. He later learned rudiments of arithmetic and geography but only in winter when he could be spared from farm chores.

At fourteen Millard was apprenticed to a cloth manufacturer in Sparta and walked there most of the hundred-mile distance from his home. The story is told that he was once sent on an errand to Dansville but lost his way, was chased by wolves and almost drowned in Canaseraga Creek. He himself has told the incident that nearly ended this apprenticeship. For some time he had been disappointed because he was forced to chop wood instead of being given an opportunity to learn the cloth-making trade. One evening after having chopped wood all day, he was told to go to the forest for more. Millard obeyed, but when his master came to watch him work, said, "I have submitted to this injustice long enough! I could learn to chop wood at home!" The older man then threatened to strike him for this insolence, at which Millard declared, "You will not chastise me. If you approach me, I will split you down!" The cloth maker silently walked away, and the next day it was agreed that Millard would be given work in the shop and stay out his alloted time.

When the three months were up, Millard walked back to Niles where he was apprenticed to a cloth maker near his home. In this situation he could study books borrowed from a circulating library while he was attending to the carding machines. Then after a term as a schoolteacher and a brief job in a sawmill, Millard had no work and hiked to visit relatives in Buffalo. Of his walk back home he later wrote, "Then for the first time I saw the rich bottom lands of the Genesee River and the beautiful village of Canandaigua, which seemed to me an earthly paradise."

Aware from his teachng experience of how little he knew, Fillmore worked for a farmer in exchange for his board so that he could attend an academy. His father then arranged with a Judge Walter Wood for Millard to study law in his office. When the young man's mother told him this news, he was so overwhelmed at the prospect of continuing his education, that he burst into tears. Not that the road ahead would be easy—he must first buy his way out of his unfinished apprenticeship to the local cloth maker, then work for the judge for seven years and eventually pay him for the privilege. But the judge once told him, "If thee has an ambition for distinction and can sacrifice everything else to success, the law is the road that leads to honors." Fillmore surely was no stranger to sacrifice.

For the next several years his law studies were interspersed with terms of teaching, but this fortunate arrangement ended suddenly when the judge forbade Fillmore to plead cases before justices of the peace because he considered this beneath the dignity of one planning to be a lawyer. Since Fillmore felt that he had to earn money this way, he regretfully broke off his relationship with the judge. He went to Aurora, where he pleaded some justice court cases and taught school; then he found a teaching position in Buffalo. There he became a clerk in a law office and once again combined his studies with schoolteaching.

Perhaps Lady Luck grew tired of so many hardships, for when he was twenty-three, Millard Fillmore's fortunes began their upward turn. Some lawyers who knew of his struggles arranged that the requirement of seven years of study be waived and that he be admitted to the bar. He first practiced law in East Aurora, then in Buffalo. Another boon was his marriage to Abigail Powers, an intelligent and cultured woman whose encouragement and good advice greatly advanced his career. After that he was successively elected to the State Assembly, to Congress, to the position of State Comptroller and the nation's Vice-President. Upon Zachary Taylor's death in 1850, he became President.

During the rest of his life, Fillmore enjoyed the role of Buffalo's first citizen. From helping draw up that city's first charter, he went on to be a founder of both its General Hospital and Historical Society, first chancellor of the University of Buffalo and a supporter of the Public Library, Fine Arts Academy and Society of Natural Sciences. On a trip to Europe he was presented to Queen Victoria, who termed him the most handsome man she had ever met. Oxford University offered him an honorary degree at that time, but Fillmore declined it. Evidently he was not out of touch with his origins, for he explained that he felt he did not deserve a degree which, being in Latin, he could not read.

SOURCES

Fillmore, Millard, *Millard Fillmore Papers*
Grayon, Benson, *The Unknown President: The Administration of Millard Fillmore*

Gov. John Young and the True Whig Spirit

Politics loomed large in nineteenth-century America, and when a hometown boy won an election, his fellow townspeople rejoiced in his success. The night in 1846 when John Young (1802–1852) won the nomination as candidate for governor was no exception. Geneseoans did not keep secret their pride in him. If the report of the *Livingston Republican* can be believed, when the special express brought the news, "one universal shout of approbation rent the air and echoed long and loud in cheers and huzzas, such as are made only at the height of unbounded joy."

A crowd quickly gathered at the American Hotel, where a meeting was held and a committee appointed to inform Young of his victory. These men came back to report that "Mr. Young was found enjoying a fine flow of spirits and received the announcement of the committee in the spirit of a true Whig." Furthermore, he accepted the nomination!

The meeting adjourned to the front of Young's house to fire a cannon and shout for joy. It then moved down the street "made light as noonday by numerous bonfires" to the Eagle Tavern, where, doubtless, spirits were consumed with more true Whig spirit. "The Whig houses were opened for the night," the newspaper account concludes, "and for once the quiet village of Geneseo gave free rein to the expression and demonstration of joy."

John Young's short but intensely active life was closely associated with Livingston County. Born in 1802 in Vermont, he came at the age of four to Conesus, where his father farmed and kept a public house. He attended the Conesus common school and is said to have memorized entire books on Greek and Roman history. His formal education ended with brief attendance at, and graduation from, Lima Academy.

At age sixteen Young taught in the Conesus common school

for nine dollars a week. Having early determined to be a lawyer, he studied in the office of an East Avon attorney for five years, supporting himself by teaching and doing apprentice legal work. After further study with a Geneseo lawyer, Young was admitted to practice before the State Supreme Court and opened an office in Geneseo in 1829. The next year he was elected town supervisor and three years later married Ellen Harris of York.

His indignation at the abduction and murder of William Morgan by the Masons led Young to join the Anti-Masonic Party. He ran for the State Assembly on that slate in 1831, won easily and was re-elected two years later. With James Wadsworth, Allen Arault and others, he supported the building of the Genesee Valley Canal. Later, having transferred his allegiance to the Whig Party, he was appointed to fill a vacancy in Congress. He afterward ran for that office and won by a wide margin.

Young served again in the State Assembly when Livingston and County Whigs elected him for two terms. His support of governmental reforms and internal improvements, such as canals and railroads, cemented his popularity. An eloquent speaker, he gradually gained leadership in the Whig Party.

If his Geneseo neighbors were elated by Young's nomination for governor, their cup overflowed when he was overwhelmingly elected in 1846. Once again a special express brought the news, and a procession marched amid cannonfire and bonfires to Young's home. He came out to hear a congratulatory speech to which he responded gracefully, and the crowd gave "three-times-three huzzas." Even after four more supporters delivered orations, the rejoicing continued into the night, presenting what the *Republican* termed "a scene of joyful enthusiasm which was emphatically gratifying to every true Whig heart."

As governor John Young supported a revision of the State constitution along more democratic lines, the completion of the Genesee Valley Canal and increased funding of the common schools and state charitable institutions. Not wishing to run for a second term, he returned to his law practice in Geneseo. Soon, however, Vice-President Millard Fillmore secured Young's appointment as Assistant Treasurer of the United States. This position took the family to New York City, where in 1852 Young died of tuberculosis at the age of forty-nine.

A biographer writing of John Young during his lifetime

described him as "a shrewd political tactition, ambitious and enterprising, determined and unyielding, frank and affable in his manner." Young's character, he thought, was "calculated to win respect and esteem and add to his considerable popularity." He added, "Who can say what other honors the future may have in store?" There were no more earthly honors for Young, but he may well be remembered as having both inspired and enjoyed celebrations in true Whig spirit.

SOURCES

Balla, Wesley, "John Young of Geneseo, New York"
Jenkins, John S., *Lives of the Governors of the State of New York*
Livingston Republican, Sept. 5, 1935

Edwin Munn, Pioneer Eye Doctor

Dr. Edwin Munn (1804–1847) rates a footnote in medical history as the second American physician to specialize in ophthalmology. By rights, he should be remembered also for his selfless service to hundreds of people suffering from eye diseases.

Having grown up in LeRoy, New York, Munn first studied with a local general practitioner, Dr. Stephen Almy, then attended the College of Physicians and Surgeons in Fairchild, New York. Beginning his practice in Scottsville in 1828, he continued the study of medicine at the University of Pennsylvania, Philadelphia, in 1834. That year he married Aristeen Pixley.

Evidently Dr. Munn first had a general practice, since a patient has recorded that whenever the doctor was riding about Scottsville and saw someone with his hand or arm tied up, he would stop to ask what was the trouble. If the person said, for instance, that he or she had broken a thumb, he would set it then and there, saying, "You can go on your way rejoicing. Your hand will be all right." His interest in eye diseases must have dated back to his work with Dr. Almy, however, for it is reported that when the older physician could not help people with sore eyes, they often turned to Munn, pleading, "Ed, for God's sake, try and help us."

"Try and help" people is what this young man did far beyond the call of duty. Early in his career, his knowledge and skill in his new specialty attracted patients from throughout New York State and beyond. Many came from long distances even though they could not afford the trip, and then Dr. Munn often paid their board bills and train fare home.

A vivid account of her experience as Dr. Munn's patient was written by Hattie Abell, who had been born blind because of cataracts. She was a young girl at the time of her treatment—a time, she said, when "people had never heard of anyone's eyes being operated on." Her parents took her to Scottsville and stayed at the Eagle Hotel where Dr. Munn came to examine her. "My mother asked if he could make me see again," she later wrote, "and he said, 'Yes, I'm going to make her see like a rat!'" This, she wrote, "braced me up a great deal."

Her father remarked that he had planned to take Hattie to New York City, but doctors there had said her eyes could not be operated on. Dr. Munn retorted that he was glad he hadn't taken the child to New York, that she would not have any sight at all if he had, that the New York doctors did not know enough to come in when it rained and that they ought to be silenced. "Colonel Abell," he declared, "if I could have seen this child earlier, I would have operated on her if she were only a day old."

Since the operation would be performed without anesthetic, Mrs. Abell urged Dr. Munn to tie Hattie's hands and feet for fear she might push him away. To this he replied, "No, I wouldn't confine her even if I were to take her head off." Telling the family that Hattie's cataracts would never recur, he began removing them, she sitting opposite him with both hands clutched around his knee. She recalled that he had an instrument which held the eyelid open and worked with one that was like a crochet needle. "He put something close around my eyes that was black as ink," she wrote. "It was to draw the pupils out so he could see better."

As for her mother's fears that the girl might move, Hattie could report, "I did not—I was so anxious to see. I do not think I would have moved if he had taken my head off."

This ordeal was but the first of nine operations on one eye and three on the other which took place over a year's time. Of the second, she wrote, "I had just as much courage then as I did the first time, and then I could see a little." In all, she was under Dr. Munn's care nearly two years. During this time, she reported, "People came from far and near to see the girl Dr. Munn had operated on and asked all sorts of questions about him. They thought I was a wonderful child to undergo the operation without being confined."

According to Hattie, the doctor "would never operate on the eye if he had been called out, and his hand might tremble. . . . He was so anxious to be successful and have me see. I never heard of anyone so anxious to be successful as he was. Why, he had a large house in Scottsville, and that house was filled with patients all the time."

As for his disposition, "He cheered everybody up when he went to see them. He would say, 'Your time hasn't come yet. You will live a long time yet.' He always had something pleasant to say and told stories to cheer a person up."

Dr. Munn moved his office to the Smith Arcade in Rochester in 1837. There his renown brought him patients from New York City and many Midwestern states, at times as many as 100 thronging his waiting room. At the end of his workday, he went to his farm in Gates. Dr. Edward Mott Moore, later surgeon-in-chief of St. Mary's Hospital, Rochester, considered him a brilliant surgeon. Studying constantly, Munn dissected eyes of animals and cadavers and experimented with surgical techniques. A newspaper account described him as humane, social and "more anxious to relieve the miserable than to amass wealth."

One recipient of his generosity was Gilbert MacBeth, who first came to Dr. Munn as a barefoot boy in ragged clothes with sore eyes. Dr. Munn took him to live with his family and in time put him through medical school. Dr. MacBeth had a successful practice in Buffalo.

After a few days of illness termed "congestion of the bowels," Edwin Munn died at age forty-three, leaving a young wife and two small children. If only he had been cared for by an internal medicine specialist half as capable as he was in his specialty!

SOURCES

Abell, Hattie, Unpublished manuscript
Hennington, C. W., "Dr. Edwin G. Munn, Rochester Ophthalmologist, As One of the Earliest Eye Specialists in America"
Rochester Democrat, Dec. 23, 1847

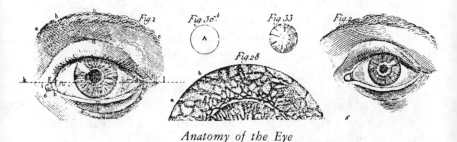

Anatomy of the Eye

Dr. James C. Jackson and Our Home on the Hill

Poor health was the blessing in disguise which set Dr. James C. Jackson (1811–1895) on a new career, leading him to establish the world-famous sanatorium, Our Home Hygienic Institution in Dansville. Though his father wanted him to follow him as a physician, young Jackson at first channeled a passion for reform into lecturing for anti-slavery societies. He and his wife, Lucretia, often sheltered escaped slaves in their Peterboro, New York, home. As a protegé of Gerrit Smith, the abolitionist leader, James progressed from editing anti-slavery journals to editing and publishing the liberal newspaper, the *Albany Patriot*.

The direction of Jackson's life changed abruptly when illness forced him to sell his paper in 1846. Beset by ailments of the heart, kidneys and digestive system, he was in his words, "broken down, shattered, shivered, lightning struck by disease and medical treatment" when he became a patient at the water cure operated by Dr. S. O. Gleason in Cuba, New York.

Dr. Gleason was a practitioner of hydropathy, a branch of medicine which treats disease by use of water. Popularized by the temperance lecturer, Sylvester Graham, who also advocated bread made from flour with the bran retained and whose name survives in the graham cracker, hydropathic sanatoriums flourished throughout the country from the 1840's to the 1890's. They espoused vegetarianism, fresh air and exercise and became associated with the temperance and women's rights movements. It is significant that Jackson included medical treatment in his list of troubles because hydropathy was one of numerous alternatives in reaction against the often ineffectual orthodox medicine of the day.

In 1847 revived by Dr. Gleason's care, Jackson went into

partnership with him and others to open Glen Haven Water Cure near Scott, New York. Having graduated from the Medical Eclectic College in Syracuse three years later, he became proprietor and physician-in-chief of the institute. A "hygienic festival" that he staged attracted 150 reform-minded persons, including Elizabeth Cady Stanton and Amelia Bloomer. True to his instincts for reform, Dr. Jackson hired as his assistant physician Harriet Austin, M.D. (1826–1891), a graduate of a New York City hydropathic institute. Her character and ability caused Dr. Jackson to adopt her as a member of his family.

After a fire which destroyed their main building, the doctors looked for a site where they could build a larger establishment. They found it in Dansville where a partially-completed water cure building had recently been abandoned. It was situated by a spring which, in 1798, had burst out of the hill east of the village with such force that it carried away trees, rocks and earth. Called "All Healing Spring," it was believed to have curative properties especially helpful in the relief of kidney and bladder diseases. In 1858 Drs. Jackson and Austin opened Our Home on the Hillside, with a friend, F. Wilson Hurd, as a shareholder. Mrs. Jackson headed the dietary and housekeeping departments, and their son, Giles, managed the business.

Begun with capitol of $750, the enterprise was an immediate success, admitting fifty patients in the first several months.

Over the next twenty-four years, the Jackson Water Cure would earn an international reputation, acquire forty acres of property and expand to accommodate 300 people at a time. Dr. Jackson was to say that he had treated more then 13,000 patients, never once dispensing a drop of medicine.

Drs. Jackson and Austin were in complete agreement that water, rather than drugs, was the natural and primary agent of cure. They prescribed cold-water baths, half-baths, sitz baths, plunges and wet-sheet wrappings, along with the drinking of copious amounts of water. They believed that conforming to the laws of health would remove the causes of disease. They based their "psycho-hygienic" treatment on the power of mind over matter, of the spiritual over the material. Besides water, their remedies were fresh air, simple food, sunlight, comfortable dress, exercise, sleep, rest, plus proper social, mental and moral influences. Since most of their patients were suffering from "overwork and nervous exhaustion" as well as "female weakness," these prescriptions were generally appropriate.

Diet was an important aspect of the regimen. Served only twice a day, meals featured fruits and vegetables with bread made from graham flour and omitted meat, fish, butter, coffee, tea and spices. Dr. Jackson invented two products: Somo, a coffee substitute, and Granula, a twice-baked mixture of graham flour and water ground into nuggets and served with milk. (A group of Seventh-Day Adventists, after a stay at Our Home, founded the Western Health Reform Institute in Battle Creek, Michigan. Its manager, Dr. John H. Kellogg, and his brother invented the remarkably similar cereal, Granose, and a patient, C. W. Post, developed the closely-related Grape Nuts.)

Comfortable clothing was recommended at the Sanatorium in reaction to the tightly-laced corsets and confining skirts then in fashion. Drs. Jackson and Austin had admired the pants outfit which Mrs. Bloomer and Mrs. Stanton had worn to the Glen Haven Water Cure hygienic festival, but Harriet designed what she consided an improvement on it. Termed the "American costume," it was a knee-length coat-dress of Prince-Albert-coat-cut worn over straight trousers. Less fussy than the Bloomer costume, if somewhat mannish, it was popular with Our Home patients and was a factor leading to simpler clothes for women. To avoid what she termed "congestion of the brain," Dr. Austin wore her hair combed straight back and cut even with the nape of the neck, but in this step she had few imitators.

Both doctors taught health habits tirelessly. Besides writing many books, Dr. Jackson gave attendance-required talks on "right living" at six-thirty every morning. Sprinkled throughout his conversation were such adages as "You must get well from within" and "Don't take tonics; take care." Dr. Austin edited the magazine, *The Laws of Life* for many years.

Yet convalescence at Our Home was not austere; the Seventh-Day Adventist leader, Ellen G. White, in fact found its cardplaying and dancing "sophistries of the devil." During their stated rest hour each day, patients lay on cots under the trees wearing white cotton skull caps kept wet with water from All Healing spring. Some rested on deck chairs wrapped in blankets or promenaded about the grounds. Picnics were enjoyed in summer, sleigh rides in winter and stereoptican viewings, lectures, poetry readings and musicales throughout the year. Founder's Day was celebrated year-ly with a full-scale program of affectionate reminiscence.

Dr. Jackson lived up to his oft-repeated motto, "A merry heart doeth good like medicine;" Dr. Harriet won loyal fans for her good sense and charming manner; and "Mother" Jackson, as she was called, dispensed tender loving care. Clara Barton was no more admiring than many another "alumna" of Our Home in asking, "Do I not owe to it all that I am?"

In 1861 the Jacksons' younger son, James H., took over the business management of the institute from Giles, who was to die of consumption three years later. When James married the former Katherine Johnson, she took over Mrs. Jackson's housekeeping duties, and her parents joined the extended family, her father becoming superintendent of buildings and grounds. Later James H. and Katherine went to New York City where he graduated from Bellevue Hospital Medical College and she from the College of New York Infirmary for Women, one of the first orthodox medical colleges for women in the nation, then directed by Dr. Emily Blackwell, sister of Dr. Elizabeth.

The younger Jackson couple then assisted his father and Dr. Austin until 1882 when the two older physicians retired and the son became physician-in-chief and sole owner of the business. His and "Dr. Kate's" son, James Arthur, was in turn the Sanatorium's business manager first and a physician later, graduating from the University of Buffalo School of Medicine only several days after the death of his grandfather. Even so, the old gentleman could have reflected at the last that he had founded quite a dynasty of physicians, including two women by adoption and marriage, and with their help had influenced countless people to "Health by right living."

SOURCES

Bunnell, A. O., *Dansville 1789-1902*
Carson, Gerald, "Bloomers and Bread Crumbs"
Conklin, William D., "The Jackson Health Resort"
"Jackson, James C.," *Dictionary of American Biography*
Numbers, Ronald L., "Dr. Jackson's Water Cure and Its Influence on Adventist Health Reform"

The Covenanters of York

The customs of the Covenanter Church, which once flourished in York, were not designed to attract converts. Rather, they expressed beliefs which the Covenanters held with stalwart determination. Officially named the Reformed Presbyterian Church in America, the denomination was called Covenanter because it adhered to the National Covenant, or agreement, adopted by Scottish Presbyterians in 1638. Before coming to this country from Scotland, these people were persecuted by the English government and sometimes even by other Scottish Presbyterians. With a certain pride, they claimed that their beliefs were both scriptural and unpopular.

Covenanters would not recognize any civil government which did not explicitly admit that it derived its powers from Jesus Christ. Thus they refused to vote, to serve on juries and to hold political office. Similarly, they would join no secret society in which members might have to swear allegiance to some institution, instead of to God. "It is not for a trifling reason," wrote one of their historians, "that we forego privileges dear to every freedman and subject ourselves to the reproach of men."

The Covenanters' doctrine was brought to the Valley in 1815 by the Rev. James Milligan, described by a colleague as "that indefatigable pioneer and missionary." Through his efforts a congregation was organized in York in 1823. The twenty-eight members first met in the barn of James Milroy northeast of the village. Two years later the first session, or governing body, was formed with James Guthrie, Sr.; James Guthrie, Jr.; James Cullings and James Milroy as ordained ruling elders.

In 1831 the group installed a pastor, the Rev. John Fisher. Services were held in Milroy's barn, in people's homes and in schoolhouses until 1834 when a church was built on West Street. Each male member found and hauled stones for it; each one who owned a horse and wagon drew a load of lumber; and those who failed in this were charged accordingly. A second church was built in 1871 on Main Street. Fifteen years later the congregation, by then numbering 200, bought a parsonage across the street from the church.

These God-fearing folk kept the Sabbath free from labor, performing all such chores as cleaning and cooking on Saturday, even walking to church in order to give their horses a day's rest each week. Their long Sunday service included two sermons and the explanation of a psalm. They practiced "fencing the table," admitting only qualified members to the Lord's Supper. With this went "table addresses," announcement of reasons why certain members were not allowed to come to the table. Another custom was the distribution of tokens which each communicant handed to an elder as he came to the table. This was a relic of the days in Scotland when it was necessary to identify bona fide members and prevent spies from infiltrating their ranks.

Covenanters sang psalms but no other songs, believing that no one had the right to substitute words of human creation for the God-given words of the Bible. Nor did they allow instrumental music in their worship. The story is told that one Sunday the elder of the York congregation who usually started the psalm-singing was absent. The man who took his place had no tuning fork, got the notes pitched too high and, when faced with a very high note, squealed, "Catch it, somebody, for I canna."

With the increasing secularization of society in the twentieth century, this group's membership dwindled—typically, its young people left when they became twenty-one and wanted to vote. The final service was held in 1931 when, as the last surviving congregation of their denomination in Western New York, they joined the United Presbyterian Church. Four years later their church was sold and torn down. But its tower was put atop the York Town Hall. There it tells the passing hours with such accuracy as to be always withing two seconds of international time, a reminder of the Covenanters' passion for truth.

SOURCES

Glasgow, W. Melancthon, *History of the Reformed Presbyterian Church in America*

Root, Mary, *History of York*

The Man Who Raised Fish by the Millions

Few people have devoted their lives so single-mindedly to one thing as did Seth Green (1817–1888). Fish were his lifelong interest from his boyhood through the years when he was internationally known for fish-breeding.

Seth was a small boy when his family moved to Carthage, a village north of Rochester on the Genesee River. There Seneca Indian playmates taught him the art of fishing, and through innate powers of observation he learned much about the habits of fish. At age twenty-one he made this enthusiasm his livelihood, catching fish to sell to crews of sailing ships which plied to and from Canada. On a fishing trip to Grafton, Ontario, Seth found the salmon entering a creek so plentiful that he fished there every year for the next thirteen years.

One time when the salmon there were about to spawn, the young man climbed a tree to observe and learn their habits. He stayed in that tree two days, an important two days in his life. He saw that when the fish cast her spawn, other fish ate the eggs, leaving only a few to hatch, and it occurred to him that such waste could be prevented by somehow hatching fish artificially.

In 1848 Green married Helen Cooke of Rochester and opened a fish market on Front Street in Rochester. His business grew to become one of the largest of its kind in the state, employing about 100 men. He also became known among sportsmen as a skillful fisherman. Though he had never heard of fish being hatched artificially, he later said, "I kept the idea constantly in my mind and took advantage of every opportunity to learn something in regard to it."

At that time a few scientists in America and Europe had artificially fertilized and incubated fish but only as laboratory experiments, not as a commercial enterprise. Green's important work began in 1864 when he bought the use of a trout pond in Caledonia and began to raise trout for stocking public streams. Caledonia's Spring Creek offered an ideal environment to trout. Springs of very pure water all along its length kept it activated and at the proper temperature, and it contained nourishing plants and insects. On a site once owned by Donald McKenzie, Caledonia settler, Green built a small hatching house along the creek. Beside it he set wooden tanks in shallow pits, their tops level with the ground.

In his first attempts to impregnate trout eggs, Green stripped female fish of their eggs and males of their milt, mixing them with water. Twenty-five per cent of the eggs hatched, a rate equal to that produced in laboratory trials. Not satisfied with this, Green experimented until he found that eggs and milt mixed without water resulted in a ninety per cent rate of success.

Soon after being fertilized, the eggs formed a hard outer coating, and Green placed them in hatching beds under running water. When they hatched after about 160 days, the tiny trout clustered together in such close contact that Green had to separate them with a feather to prevent their suffocating. The fish fed off umbilical sacs containing nourishment for thirty days, after which Green fed them finely-sieved beef liver. Ten days later he could turn them loose into his pond and thence to the creek. As his accomplishments became widely known, he sold trout spawn for ponds across the country.

At the invitation of authorities of four New England states, Green went to Holyoke, Massachusetts, in 1867 to attempt to propagate shad. After many trials and errors, he learned how their requirements differed from those of trout and tirelessly adjusted environmental conditions to match the natural process. It made this arduous work even more difficult when a group of fishermen, thinking that an abundance of shad would lower its price, played every imaginable trick to ruin his experiments. But just before the spawning season ended, Green succeeded, producing shad with less trouble and more certainty than trout. Before leaving Holyoke, he had placed 40,000,000 shad in the Connecticut River.

Appointed one of a three-man New York State fishing commission in 1869, Green built the State's hatching house at Caledonia where trout, salmon, whitefish and shad were propagated. Since New York's rivers were becoming depleted, he began to re-stock the Hudson near Coeymans. Fishermen there understood his work so little (and may have thought his dedication to his task so strange) that they thought he was insane.

Later as the State's Superintendent of Fish Culture, he supplied free fish to any person willing to stock a body of public water which was becoming depleted. He established a hatchery at Cold Spring Harbor, Long Island, where the rare grayling was successfully reared. Meanwhile problems of aeration, temperature, feeding and transportation were overcome. An important contribution to Eastern fishing was his introduction from Germany of brown trout, making fishing possible in streams unfavorable to other species. Green also put many thousands of perch, bass, herring, sturgeon and catfish in the Potomac as well as shad in many Southeastern United States rivers.

As his fame spread to California, its commissioners wrote to ask if he could send them shad. Green replied that newly-hatched shad living off their umbilical sacs might possibly survive and that he would try to transport them by train. Carrying four eight-gallon milk cans containing 12,000 just-hatched shad, he began his trip at the Hudson. When he arrived in Cleveland, he poured 200 fish into Lake Erie and changed the remaining fish's water. Reaching Chicago, he provided Lake Michigan with 200 specimens in exchange for fresh water. He acquired water in Omaha but, testing it on a few of his little charges, found that it killed them. Worse, he could not get a full change of water for the next 400 miles of the train ride.

"It was a blue time for me," he said later. "I would look at the helpless little fellows; they were suffering and so was I. I had brought them into the world and would not see them suffer if it was possible for me to help them." Then he thought of the drinking water in the railroad cars and began taking it to his pets in the baggage car. At this use of the passengers' drinking water, the baggage man became violently abusive. But he was persuaded to see reason in Green's explanation when it was accompanied by a generous donation. Similar contributions soon had all the porters carrying water for the cause until Green could say, "My little fish began to stop rolling up their big eyes at me, and I was happy." Soon another danger threatened—extremely hot weather meant that Green had to add ice to the water in minute amounts in order to keep its temperature below eighty-two degrees. After seven days and nights of this vigil, Seth and his fish reached Sacramento where the fish commissioners conducted them to the river. But all was not yet well, for Green pronounced the river too turbulent at that place, and the group traveled to its source. There they deposited about 1,000 shad, the first to live in a tributary of the Pacific Ocean. In time these multiplied to such numbers that fishermen limited their catches of shad to keep from overstocking the market.

At the Caledonia hatchery Green experimented with crossing striped bass with shad, shad with herring, brook trout with herring, brook trout with California salmon, salmon trout with whitefish and European trout with American brook trout. He wrote many articles for both technical and sporting publications and three books, *Trout Culture*, *Home Fishing in Home Waters* and, in collaboration with his life-long friend, Robert B. Roosevelt (uncle of President Theodore Roosevelt), *Fish Hatching and Fish Catching*. Societies in the United States, France and Germany honored him with gold medals.

It has been said that Seth Green's work made modern fishing possible. But even more than his work Seth Green loved fishing. His name lives on in his invention of a tackle, the Seth Green rig. Perhaps his favorite of the many tributes paid him would be this from Robert Roosevelt:

> But of all positions the one in which he most shines is when he is wielding the light but powerful flyrod that he loves and understands so well. He gazes far off over the circled water looking after the falling of his fly as time after time he lifts the long line with a powerful yet elegant motion and, swinging it far behind him, casts it forward with the perfection of easy force. That is his forte, and few may dare to enter the lists against him.

SOURCES

Black, Sylvia, "Seth Green, Father of Fish Culture"
"Green, Seth," *Dictionary of American Biography*
Seth Green and the Caledonia Fish Hatchery

Frederick Douglass's Moral Victory

Frederick Douglass (c.1817–1895) made two escapes to freedom. The first was a physical escape—his flight from bondage to a Maryland slave owner in 1838. Three years later he attended a Massachusetts Anti-Slavery Society convention at which he spoke so effectively that he was hired to lecture for the society. He quickly formed friendships with William Lloyd Garrison and other New England abolitionists.

Paradoxically, his success as a speaker for the cause led to trouble, for telling his experiences put him in risk of being recaptured. To avoid identifying his former master, he blurred some details of his earlier life. This vagueness caused many of his hearers to suspect he was a fraud. They refused to believe that one so few years beyond slavery could speak so learnedly. Resenting their charges, Douglass began to speak on even more intellectual matters and so became increasingly unpopular.

"Just tell your own story," one Anti-Slavery official advised him, while another suggested that he include "a little more plantation speech." Douglass refused and went so far as to write his autobiography, complete with incriminating facts. Then in danger of being captured, he went to England in 1845.

When Douglass returned after two years, he found that his relationship with Garrison and his fellow-workers had worsened. Their chief disagreement lay in Douglass's wish to found an abolitionist newspaper and in Garrison's fear that he was not capable of such an undertaking. While in England, Douglass had become used to being fully accepted in white society, but with Garrison's circle he felt he was merely a symbol of the anti-slavery cause. He later observed of his first experience with them, "For a time I was made to forget that my skin was dark and my hair crisped." But as the historian, Peter Walker, has noted, "He was

scarcely freed from white people . . . He had ceased to be a Negro
. . . He was meant to play a particular role in the Garrisonians'
establishment. He was intended to be a specimen." He was a token
Black.

Frederick Douglass made his second escape in 1847 by
moving to Rochester where he founded the newspaper, *The North
Star*. The change in his life was such that within months, James
McCune Smith, Black physician and writer, said of him, ". . . only
since his editorial career has he seen fit to become a colored man!
He is as one newly born among us."

Despite some instances of race prejudice in his early years
there, Douglass felt at home in Rochester. He described it as "the
center of a virtuous, intelligent, enterprising, liberal and growing
population." Looking back on the move, he wrote, "I know of no
place in the Union where I could have located at the time with less
resistance or received a larger measure of sympathy and coopera-
tion." He found abolitionists of the area more liberal than those in
New England, and during the life of his journal from 1847 until
1863 had the support of such men as Gerrit Smith, Charles
Sumner, William Seward, Horace Mann and Salmon P. Chase.

What must have pleased him were invitations to lecture on
subjects other than race relations. He took part in the first wom-
en's rights convention held in 1848 and also addressed the
Rochester Temperance Society. At such times he was regarded as a
person in his own right, rather than as a symbol.

Over the years Douglass became a leading spokesman for his
people's freedom. He was prominent in the Underground Railroad
through which hundreds of slaves were moved on to Canada.
During the war he recruited Blacks for the Union army and
afterward worked for their civil rights.

In 1895 after having moved to Washington where he served
in several governmental appointments, Douglass died in his late
seventies. On the last day of his life he took part in a women's
suffrage convention, working for the freedom of all humans.

SOURCES

Douglass, Frederick, *Life and Times Written by Himself*
Sterling, Philip, and Logan, Rayford, *Four Took Freedom*
Quarles, Benjamin, comp., *Frederick Douglass*
Walker, Peter F., *Moral Choices: Memory, Desire and Imagination in Nineteenth-century Abolition*
Washington, Booker T., *Frederick Douglass*

Lewis H. Morgan, "One Lying Across"

Sometimes called "the father of American anthropology," Lewis H. Morgan (1818–1881) was also once rated "the most eminent Rochesterian of the nineteenth century." Though he devoted most of his career to the law, his fame rests on his study of Indian culture, which developed out of a youthful hobby and a chance meeting.

After graduating from Union College in Schenectady, Lewis returned to his home, Aurora, New York, to study law. There he and some friends formed a secret society called "The Grand Order of the Iroquois." Half in earnest and half in fun, the young men wore Indian dress during "councils" held by firelight in the woods. Wanting to learn more about the Iroquois, Lewis went to Albany to study Indian treaties in 1844. While browsing in a bookstore, he became acquainted with Ely S. Parker, a Seneca chief who would later become a member of General Grant's staff and Commissioner of Indian Affairs.

Here was a source of the very knowledge Lewis craved. Questioning Ely, he learned much about the social structure of the League of Six Nations: Senecas, Mohawks, Oneidas, Onondagas, Cayugas and Tuscaroras. The two quickly became close friends, Lewis helping Ely to enter the Cayuga Academy in Aurora and Ely explaining traditional Indian customs. Under Morgan's leadership, the Grand Order of the Iroquois became dedicated to the study and perpetuation of Indian culture.

Representing the Grand Order and a Batavia citizen's group, Morgan went to Washington in 1846 to help defeat a bill which would have given the Ogden Land Company property rightly belonging to the Senecas. In gratitude, the Hawk Clan adopted him, giving him the same name that they had earlier bestowed on

Horatio Jones: Ta-ya-da-o-woh-koh, meaning "One Lying Across," a link between two peoples.

After being admitted to the bar, Morgan married and worked with a Rochester lawyer in 1851. Meanwhile he continued his study of Iroquois society—now with increased urgency because ancient structures of government were being replaced by white customs, and knowledge of them could soon be lost. That year saw publication of Morgan's *The League of Ho-de-no-sau-nee, or Iroquois*, the first systematic study of an Indian tribe, which he dedicated to Ely Parker. To a public which dismissed Indians as ignorant savages, he portrayed them as "bound together by permanent institutions, governed by fixed laws and guided by well-established usages and customs."

Morgan founded the Rochester literary society named "the Club" and nicknamed "the Pundit Club," at which he presented thirty-four scholarly paper over the years. As early as 1852 he tried to establish a college for women in Rochester, saying, "There is no reason why female education should not be as thorough . . . as it is in our colleges." Though he was helped in this effort by James S. Wadsworth of Geneseo among others, he could not raise enough funds for so radical a concept. He did, however, serve as a trustee of Wells College for the Higher Education of Young Women in Aurora from its founding in 1868 until his death. Perhaps in this work he had in mind his two daughters, who had died of scarlet fever, a disease which also left his son severely disabled. During 1860's he was a member of both the State Assembly and the Senate.

As legal advisor of a Michigan railroad, Morgan not only acquired wealth but also extended his study of Indian lore to tribes of the Midwest. On holidays he took fishing trips in the northern Michigan wilderness where there were almost no humans but many thousand beavers. The result of his observations was *The Beaver*, a study of beaver psychology and sociology showing their ability to work cooperatively, plan ahead, reason and meet emergencies. A reviewer has said of it, "One is almost persuaded that the book was written by a beaver. Only a beaver could speak so knowingly about beavers."

Among Morgan's many learned writings on Indians are the geographical and explanatory notes to J. E. Seaver's *Life of Mary*

Jemison which are included in the book's fourth and all later editions. His wider research into the customs of many Indian tribes dealt with the similarity of their traditions, including descent reckoned from the maternal line, chiefs chosen by both heredity and election and government by tribal councils. Pioneering in the study of kinship terminology, he concluded that the kinship systems of all the tribes in America were nearly the same.

Morgan published his major work, *Ancient Society*, in 1877. In it he asserted the common origin of all races of men. In his search for universal principles of cultural evolution, he saw a law of inevitable social progress. This concept of social evolution as well as his notion that societies necessarily move from the primitive to the civilized have since been discredited, but they were advances upon the opinion of his time. And his basic approach to social institutions has influenced all anthropology since then.

For all his abstruse labors, Lewis Morgan was a sociable man and a leader in Rochester's intellectual circle. He was a close friend of Charles A. Dewey, M.D.; Dr. William W. Ely; Rev. Algernon Crapsey and a multitude of young students. He was the first organizer of the Rochester Historical Society, the first to suggest a Rochester Academy of Science and later a member of the National Academy of Sciences. He helped organize the Section of Anthropology of the American Association for the Advancement of Science and in 1879 was president of the whole Association.

Lewis Morgan willed his estate for the lifetime use of his wife and son, the residue to go to the University of Rochester for the education of women. Thus his efforts, begun half a century before, united with those of Susan B. Anthony and her friends to admit women in 1900. There were two ways in which he lived up to his Indian name of "a bridge between two groups."

SOURCES

Armstrong, William H., *Warrior in Two Camps*: *Ely S. Parker*

Crapsey, Algernon S., "Lewis Henry Morgan, Scientist, Philosopher, Humanist"

Dewey, Charles A., "Sketch of the Life of Lewis Henry Morgan with Personal Reminiscences"

Gilchrist, Donald, "Bibliography of Lewis Henry Morgan"

Holmes, William Henry, "Biographical Memoir of Lewis Henry Morgan"

Holtzman, S. F., "Lewis Henry Morgan"

McIlvaine, Rev. J. H., "Life and Works of Lewis Henry Morgan, L.L.D., An Address at His Funeral"

"Morgan, Lewis Henry," *Dictionary of American Biography*

Slater, John R., "Lewis Henry Morgan"

Susan B. Anthony to the Rescue

While not generally supporting Susan B. Anthony (1820–1906), the people of Rochester were coming to respect her by the 1890's. It had been a long fight. As far back as in 1852 when she demanded the right to speak at a temperance rally, respectable Rochesterians thought her unbecomingly aggressive. Such rebuffs only strengthened Miss Anthony's belief that until women gained equal rights they could not achieve other social reforms.

For forty years this "Napoleon of the woman's rights movement" stumped the country in tireless, single-minded and dedicated pursuit of women's suffrage. As the leader of the feminist movement, she had attracted reams of ridicule in the nation's press, but by the 1890's such attacks had moderated. As she said, the typical legislator had earlier confronted her "with a smirk on his face as though he considered woman's rights nonsensical, but now public men look upon our mission as a matter of business."

One item of business on Miss Anthony's agenda was higher education for women. A teacher in her youth, she had insisted on the right to speak at a Teachers' Association meeting in 1852. Having returned to Rochester to live with her sister, Mary, in 1891, she set out to help open the University of Rochester to women. During a visit from Elizabeth Cady Stanton, the pair called a meeting with the University's president of the Board of Trustees to urge coeducation. They got only as far as making their cause a story for the newspapers, but there were some sympathetic cartoons, which encouraged them.

For seven more years the Anthony sisters, members of the local Political Equality Club and other women's groups kept the subject before the public in speeches and resolutions. It was not to Rochester's credit, they claimed, that its young women had to go away for a college education when both the University of Michigan and Cornell had admitted women since the seventies. Furthermore, the University had an obligation to educate women, since Lewis Henry Morgan had willed it funds for that purpose. At this time women could sit in on a class in art and one in poetry, but received no credit.

Finally the trustees opened the door a crack. If $100,000 could be raised within a year, a limited number of women would be admitted As a member of the fund-raising committee, Anthony knew such an effort would divert money from suffrage, her foremost cause, but believed that coeducation was worth the sacrifice. The women found their work hard going, especially since a campaign to build a gymnasium being conducted at the same time was far more popular with the University's alumni. When their year was ended in 1899, the women persuaded the trustees to reduce the required amount to $50,000 and extend the deadline another year.

Although the club members worked harder, they found the city's financiers, notably George Eastman, unreceptive, and the great majority of the alumni opposed to their goal. In these months Miss Anthony, having many other concerns, left the fund-raising largely to others. She had just returned from a long trip when she received alarming news from the committee's secretary. Their deadline was the very next day; every conceivable source had been approached but they were $8,000 short of $50,000; and she was the only other committee member then in town. Susan B. Anthony slept little that night.

Next morning she began with her sister, who she knew planned to will the University $2,000 for women's education. "Give it now,"she begged. "Don't wait, or the girls may never be admitted." With $6,000 to go, she and a friend took a carriage to homes, stores, offices and factories about the city, calling on many who had already given, and so raised all but the last $2,000. This was the hardest, for they met with many refusals. After one very wealthy woman had apologized for not contributing because of her many expenses, Susan exclaimed in exasperation, "Thank heaven I am not as poor as she is!"

Meanwhile the trustees were meeting and apt to adjourn at any moment. In desperation Susan called on an old friend who had given generously before, only to learn he felt he had done all he could. She then asked if he would guarantee the amount until she could raise it, and he agreed. Hurrying to the Granite Building, the exhausted but triumphant women reported that they had pledges for the full $50,000. The trustees, investigating the pledges, objected to the final one for $2,000 because the guarantor was ill and there was doubt that upon his death his estate would fulfill hs wish. "Gentlemen, I may as well confess" was Miss Anthony's response. "I am the guarantor." She explained that she had asked the old gentleman to lend his name so that coeducation would not suffer by being associated with women's suffrage. "I now pledge my life insurance for the $2,000," she added.

After an agonizing wait of two more days while the trustees reviewed the pledges, Susan could write in her diary, "They let the girls in. He said there was no alternative." Later the women of the fund-raising committee made up the $2,000 and returned her life insurance policy to her.

SOURCES

Anthony, Katharine, *Susan B. Anthony*
Harper, Ida H., *Life and Work of Susan B. Anthony*
Lutz, Alma, *Susan B. Anthony*
McKelvey, Blake, *Rochester, The Quest for Quality*

The Unofficial Clara Barton

"Angel of the battlefield," "mother of the world," "America's Florence Nightingale"—these are some of the accolades heaped upon Clara Barton (1821–1912). She has been so closely identified with the American Red Cross that it is hard to picture her as a flesh-and-blood person. Actually, she was a warmly emotional woman with a love of fun. Her human qualities are especially evident in her fondness for Dansville and its people.

Though her work often took her away from it, Dansville was home to Miss Barton from 1876 to 1886. Ten years earlier, she had visited it briefly to lecture on her experience of ministering to Union casualties in the Civil War. Later in Europe she had learned of the International Red Cross, an agency established to provide for the neutrality of persons and materials aiding ill or wounded servicemen. After helping victims of the Franco-Prussian War, she returned to her home in Massachusetts, in her words, "an almost hopeless invalid." (The term, "semi-invalid," would probably be a more accurate description of this ninety-pound woman who was, no doubt, physically and emotionally exhausted from her gruelling war work.)

When a friend recommended that she go to the Jackson Water Cure in Dansville, Miss Barton recalled having heard of it during her stay there in 1866 and applied for admission. In case she might not find everything about it to her liking, she arranged with the help of the Dansville postmaster to rent a house on Leonard Street in the village. But Clara spent little time there, so delighted was she with Dr. James C. Jackson's and Dr. Harriet Austin's water cure, Our Home Hygienic Institution. "Their place is simply beautiful," she wrote. "I never saw together any group of people that combine the degrees of intellect, general intelligence and culture as is collected here ... The people are very kind and social. There is no stiffness." Years later she was to tell Dr. Jackson that it was worth all her illness to have known his Sanatorium.

Clara quickly formed what was to become a life-long friendship with Dr. Austin. For a short time she wore "the American Costume," a coat-dress and pants outfit which the doctors had originated as a more attractive alternative to the Bloomer suit, in protest against current female fashions. Wearing it as many Sanatorium patients did, Miss Barton reported that she was dressed "as free and easy as a gentleman, perambulating around to suit myself." She joined in the frivolity of a "Betsy Bobbet" club whose members took on the names of characters in a series of humorous books then popular. She found an excursion to Rochester which the group made "no end of fun."

Recuperated in her second year in Dansville, Miss Barton began her crusade to bring about United States affiliation with the International Red Cross. She first rented a house on Leonard and Elizabeth Streets where she lived five years. There she enjoyed gardening, canning fruit and entertaining. There, too, her cat, Tommy, reigned, as she said, "pretty much master of the house." Joining the Coterie, a local literary club, she presented toasts to honorary members at one meeting and lectured on the Franco-Prussian War at another. Through her interest in the Dansville Seminary, a boarding and day school, she met Dr. Julian B. Hubbell, who later became her field agent in relief work and devoted co-worker. As she carried on her arduous efforts to bring the United States into the International Red Cross, this very human woman must sometimes have tired of the weight of her public image, as when Dr. Jackson introduced her as "one of the most remarkable women of this or any age."

The women of Dansville showed their support for the celebrity who was also their friend and neighbor when she was nearly sued as a horse thief. As a Dansville woman recounted the incident, Clara was suddenly summoned one morning to go to a lawyer's office where she was to be put on trial. Soon she and "a goodly number of ladies" filled the office and learned that the plaintiff was an ignorant man who, knowing of Miss Barton's usual generosity, had often tried to sell her an aged horse. One day he hitched it at her door, leaving word that she should give him her decision later.

When evening came but the owner did not and Miss Barton

could not reach him, she had grass cut and the horse fed, watered and bedded in an improvised stall. The next she knew of the matter was to learn that she was being sued. When the lawyer came to his office that morning, he "fairly fell against the door" to see so many women awaiting him. "Disgusted as we all were with him," one of them wrote, "we could not but pity a man who could take such a case against our loved friend."

On May 21, 1881 Clara Barton formed the American Red Cross in Washington, D. C. Later that year members of the Coterie and citizens representing all the town's religious groups, stating that they wanted both to compliment Clara Barton and to do honor to themselves, proposed to form the nation's first local society of the Red Cross. Following a preliminary meeting at which Miss Barton explained the nature of Red Cross societies, they met in the Lutheran Church on August 22 and organized the Dansville Society, later re-named Clara Barton Chapter, No. 1.

The day came in 1886 when Miss Barton left Dansville for the last time to live in Washington. At a farewell reception she told her "beloved neighbors," "To the restfulness of your valleys and the strength of your hills, I am grateful . . . From now to the end I shall remember."

SOURCES

Clara Barton and Dansville
Williams, Blanche C., *Clara Barton*

William P. Letchworth's Useful Life

The life of William Pryor Letchworth (1823–1910) mirrors the social history of nineteenth-century America. There is little evidence of an identity crisis in this man's experience; rather, he was much in tune with his time. Letchworth's inner drives seem to have harmonized with societal pressures to shape his career.

When he was a boy, Will heard of the unhealthful working conditions of London's chimney-sweeps and contrived a plan to relieve their plight. He devised a brush based on the principle of the extension fishing rod which could be pushed upward from the bottom of the chimney. He was sure that this invention would reap him a fortune, and he dreamed of bestowing it on his family. A novelist could not have imagined a fantasy more prophetic of Letchworth's later interest in social work, invention, business enterprise and philanthropy.

Raised in the village of Sherwood near Auburn, New York, young William absorbed the values of rural America. His ancestors had been Quakers, one an early opponent of slavery, and he followed their example in his lifelong faith in God and concern for social justice. His father was respected in the community and a friend of William Seward. While attending the common school, William helped in his father's harness-making business. At age fifteen he worked for a saddlery hardware maker in Auburn, receiving his keep and forty dollars a year, from which he saved two dollars. That year he composed a list of "rules of conduct" including the injunction, "Attempt great things and expect great things."

In 1848 William began work for an affiliate of the Auburn saddlery hardware firm in New York City. There he first saw the rapid population growth, urban crowding and technological advances being brought about by the Industrial Revolution. Made a partner of the Buffalo hardware firm, Pratt and Letchworth, in 1848, he contributed to this transition for the next twenty-three years. Thanks to its position at the end of the Erie Canal and on the shore of Lake Erie, Buffalo prospered and mushroomed in those years. As Letchworth helped build his company into a leading manufacturer of fine hardware and later of carriages, he took part in America's shift from an agricultural to an industrial economy. After inventing a way to produce malleable iron, he founded the Buffalo Malleable Iron Works which made locomotive parts for the Union Army during the Civil War. This made Letchworth wealthy, but work-oriented though he was, he was not a typical "baron of industry" in that he did not consider business success an end in itself. He later said, that he had once narrowly escaped death in a carriage accident and believed that God must have spared his life for something more than making money. In 1871 aged forty-eight, he retired from Pratt and Letchworth.

A friend once said of this man, "All his life he tried to better things that needed bettering." In this he reflected the concept that man can be made perfect which led to the many social reforms of the 1800's. In 1872 Letchworth was appointed to the State Board of Charities, an unpaid committee which was the forerunner of the State Department of Social Services. He devoted most of his time and energy to this work until 1896, serving as Board president for ten years. When he saw that pauper children sentenced to the Erie County Poorhouse were subjected to unwholesome influences, he vowed, "If God will spare my life, I will not rest until these children are removed from this poisoned atmosphere." Investigating and reporting on conditions in every poorhouse in the state, he in time effected laws which transferred dependent children to orphan asylums and years later led to such children being placed in the care of families.

In visiting State institutions, Letchworth saw barbaric practices in treating the mentally ill. After studying advanced treatment methods in European mental institutions, he wrote *The Insane in Foreign Countries*, which together with his lobbying efforts, led to more humane practices. One such was the requirement that harmless patients be housed separately from the violently and criminally insane. He soon formulated this principle of proper classification of people in institutions and worked to see it implemented throughout his career.

Letchworth next brought about the separation of minor offenders from hardened criminals in juvenile reformatories. He also urged that reformatory inmates be taught useful trades; Industry, outside Rochester, is one example of this effort. In addition, he supported prison reform, temperance and women's rights.

In the 1890's Letchworth took up the cause of epileptics, who were then institutionalized with the mentaly ill. Assigned to recommend the site for a State institution for epileptics, he was largely responsible for the State's buying the Shakers' property at Sonyea in Groveland. He researched the subject of epilepsy so thoroughly that his book, *The Care and Treatment of Epileptics*, was the standard text of the time. Craig Colony was built on a principle which Letchworth had long advocated, the "cottage system." In place of huge, fortress-like buildings, the patients were housed in small groups superintended by staff members in a family-like atmosphere.

Letchworth found relief from these serious matters at Glen Iris, his estate on the Genesee at Portage. The land when he first saw it in 1858 had been devastated by lumbering operations. But the beauty of the river winding through the valley, down torrential falls and between deep canyon walls cried out to him to restore the landscape as nature had created it. He first bought land by the Middle Falls, making a house that stood there his vacation home, then later enlarged the house and lived there year around. Gradually buying adjoining properties, he eventually owned 1,000 acres where he supervised extensive landscaping. He also operated several farms and raised purebred Shorthorn cattle.

To this oasis of peace and beauty, Letchworth often invited friends and relatives, and after his sister, Mary Ann Crozer, came to live with him, it was even more a place of generous hospitality. From the first, Letchworth planned that Glen Iris would one day be used for some charitable purpose; meanwhile the public could visit and picnic on the grounds freely, and children from Buffalo Orphan Asylums could spend idyllic summers there.

By the second half of the century, evidences of past Indian and pioneer life were fast disappearing. To preserve them from falling into ruin, Letchworth had an historic Seneca council house as well as a house that Mary Jemison had built moved to his grounds. When Mary Jemison's grave was in danger of being obliterated, he had her remains re-buried and marked by a monument with a statue of the "White Woman of the Valley" carrying her baby on her back. He installed artifacts and mementos of the Valley's past in a museum open to the public.

A project which gladdened his heart was the "last council," a meeting of reconciliation that he arranged between Senecas and Mohawks, who had been estranged since the War of 1812. Gathered around a fire in the council house, descendants of Red Jacket, Cornplanter, Mary Jemison and others spoke sadly of by-gone days when their fathers "knew not the value of the soil and little imagined that the white people would cover the land as thickly as the trees from ocean to ocean." The leaders of the two nations clasped hands in friendship.

The white people present gave speeches in their turn, after which ex-President Millard Fillmore presented each Indian with Letchworth's gift of a silver medal commemorating the occasion. It was a surprise to Letchworth when later that day the Senecas called him outside his house to take part in a ceremony of adoption into the Wolf Clan. He was named Hai-wa-ye-is-ta, meaning "the man who always does the right thing."

To all but his family and close friends, Letchworth appeared the picture of Victorian reserve and formality. Yet under an assumed name he wrote three sentimental romances; he was chivalrous to women (though he never married) and loved the company of children; and he had many lasting friendships with people ranging from United States Presidents to ragged youths. Also hidden behind his sober facade was a bubbling sense of humor.

Letchworth lived from the time when settlers had to rid their land of trees to the start of the conservation movement. Seeing cities encroaching on the countryside, he zealously guarded the primal growth of Glen Iris. He was eighty years old and partially paralyzed when the falls of Glen Iris were threatened with extinction. Corporate investors tried to have the power of the falls diverted to provide Rochester with hydroelectricity. Letchworth did everything in his power to save his beloved falls. In a legal battle lasting the last seven years of his life, he lobbied the Legislature and the press to preserve this natural wonder. Finally, he put the estate into the custody of the American Scenic and Historic Preservation Society and deeded it to New York State as a park for its people. He spent many happy hours on plans for the park to become an arboretum and "an outdoor school" of the natural sciences.

Still hopeful and optimistic, Letchworth wrote some notes on the day he died about an organization which would help young working people. Many who knew him were fond of saying that he was faultless, which he was not. But he did live what in his day was admiringly called a "useful" life.

SOURCES

Beale, Irene A., *William P. Letchworth: A Man for Others*

Council Hill, Glen Iris

The Classic Halls of Temple Hill Academy

The Temple Hil Academy brought prestige to Geneseo for more than half a century, attracting students from every state and many countries. Picturing it today in its pastoral setting by the Temple Hill grove, one can hardly imagine it as a subject of controversy. Yet when it was incorporated in 1827, many Geneseoans objected to its being located in their village, and thirty years later it figured in a local church schism.

First named the Livingston County High School, it was built on two acres given by James and William Wadsworth with additional funds raised by public subscription. Among the incorporators were the Wadsworths, William and Daniel Fitzhugh, Charles Carroll and George Hosmer. James Wadsworth also donated a three-story brick classroom building and a similar dormitory to accommodate 280 students. These cost him $9,500, and a barn and outbuildings $500.

The school's prospectus described it as a collegiate institution on the monitorial system. The latter phrase refers to the system whereby students chosen from the introductory, junior and senior divisions were appointed monitors and helped their fellow-pupils with their lessons. The school was planned for young men who did not want college training for the traditional professions but who wanted more education than could be obtained in the common schools. With a mixture of idealism and practicality typical of the Genesee gentry, the founders aimed to "combine classical instruction with that of the useful arts—and at a moderate expense."

Who could find fault with that? Many could—first, because the planners had purposely avoided affiliating with any one religious denomination. Furthermore, the three faculty members appointed for the school's opening in October, 1827, had graduated that year from Harvard. Indignant citizens circulated a protest against hiring men from a college "known as a fountain of the most destructive heresy, which renders it extremely probable that they are deeply imbued with Unitarian sentiments."

The school's first principal, C. E. Felton, confided in a letter, "The good people of the village would not let their schoolmaster board with us through fear that he might become a conductor of the poisonous influence from our school to his. Some look upon us as Deists and some as worse than Atheists, and we are as much stared at as if we were unheard-of animals from the center of the earth."

Actually, the school required that all pupils attend church on the Sabbath. Parents stated whether their children should attend the Presbyterian, Episcopal or Methodist church, these being the only ones in the village. Headmaster Felton's letter continued, "I am the chaplain of the establishment and read from the Episcopal service morning and evening and preside over the dinner table. You would laugh at the difference between me now, a man of business, and a few days ago a reckless student!" This former "reckless student," then nineteen years old, went on to become an eminent Greek scholar and eventually president of Harvard.

The younger boys were taught reading, writing, spelling, geography, history and arithmetic and the older onces Greek, Latin, French, Spanish, higher mathematics, natural philosophy and chemistry. The tuition cost, varying with the grade, ranged from twelve to twenty-eight dollars a year, with board at a dollar and a quarter a week. Pupils brought not only their own linen but also their bedsteads. Teacher's salaries ranged from $240 to $400 per year.

In 1834 the school participated in New York State's first program of teacher training and thus became a forerunner of the Geneseo Normal School and the present State University College. It was one of the schools to which the State gave books and equipment to train future elementary school teachers. A Ladies Department was formed in 1841, and in the next year a class of thirty-five men and women graduated. Nearly all were employed that fall, their salaries ranging from fourteen to twenty-two dollars a month plus board. Largely to help these future teachers, James Wadsworth that year underwrote the cost of the Genesee Atheneum, predecessor to the Wadsworth Library. It made available to them, as well as to all county residents, books, scientific equipment and mineral specimens—a rare privilege in the days when libraries were open only to their subscribers.

Though usually called Temple Hill Academy, Livingston County High School never was named that; it was re-named the Geneseo Academy in 1846. Three years later it was acquired by the Presbyterian Synod of Buffalo. Again it avoided sectarianism, requiring only that the Bible be read at morning and evening worship and that pupils attend some church on Sundays.

The school's heyday occurred in the 1850's, when 400 attended in one term. They came from as far away as the Sandwich Islands and Japan. One alumnus became commander-in-chief of Japan's war against Russia. Another was Captain Horace Bixby who taught Mark Twain to be a Mississippi River pilot. Others were Gov. Washington Hunt; Charles, Craig and James W. Wadsworth; Lockwood L. Doty; William H. C. Hostner; Horatio Jones's son Charles; Dr. Henry Piffard; Henry Ward and John H. McNaughton.

Schoolchildren then were as full of mischief as they are today. One time many of them had fictitious business cards printed which they used to send for catalogues and free samples, each hall competing to see which could get the most. The goods and literature arrived in such quantities that they had to be delivered in drays. When the Geneseo postmaster complained to the school authorities, all the printed matter went into a huge bonfire around which the boys held a whooping war dance. Fruit trees and grapevines on neighboring lots were sometimes stripped overnight; donkeys were known to wander through the halls; and a wagonload of wood left in the grove somehow appeared on the school's roof. There was an ongoing feud between the Academy boys, called by their enemies "Dudes," and the town boys, called by theirs "Toughs." When the Dudes soaked their snowballs in icewater, the Toughs retaliated with stones inside theirs. And, as it will ever be, the pupils complained about the food.

Overlooking such details, an observer wrote of the school, "The renown of its classic halls, delightful retreats, balmy groves, able corps of instructors and long line of eminent and distinguished graduates throughout the land will for all time gild the historian's page."

The Academy was again the subject of dispute when it appeared that the State might establish a Normal School in Geneseo.

In 1858 local Presbyterians were divided on the issue. Those who opposed having a school which would rival the Academy left their parish and formed another. Situating the Normal School there did in fact bring about the Academy's decline, and it was closed in 1890. The so-called Old School and New School Churches were reunited in 1880.

The Academy buildings were used as storehouses until they were bought by Mr. and Mrs. Henry Colt, who had one torn down and the other remodelled into a residence in 1908. It was bought in 1942 by Dr. and Mrs. John Lockhart, Jr., who preserved the beauty of the house and grounds, which—as was once said of the school itself—are "an ornament to the village."

SOURCES

Jennings, Samuel T., Scrapbook
Livingston County Historical Society, *Annual Report, 1918*
Livingston Republican, Oct. 26, 1865; March 1, 1877; Feb. 6, 1902; Jan. 1, 1920
"Temple Hill, Geneseo, N. Y.," In *A Day in the Historic Genesee Valley*

Lockwood L. Doty's Brush with the Law

Lockwood L. Doty (1827–1873) did more in his lifetime of forty-six years than most people do in a much longer span. Beginning as a clerk in the Geneseo law office of John Young, he went with him to Albany when Young became governor. This launched him on a varied career, which included public service, executive positions with railroads and editing and publishing the *Livingston Republican*. In addition, historians have been indebted to him ever since he compiled the first history of Livingston County.

But there was one event in his youth when he must have thought that his future career might be doomed. It happened in 1842 when he was known in Dansville as "the Doty boy from Groveland." He had come there several years before and was now deputy postmaster.

The story is told by Doty's friend, young Augustus Gilbert. It begins when a neighboring shopkeeper, a Mr. McVicker, went into Augustus' father's store and asked for a ten dollar bill in exchange for ten dollars in coins. McVicker folded the bill in a paper, sealed it with a wafer, or sticker, addressed it and placed it in his hat after which Augustus saw him go into his shop next door.

Several days later someone came into the Gilberts' store to announce, "The United States marshall has arrested Lock Doty! He's taking him to Rochester on the canal packet which has just left. The marshall searched him and then took him off. All he would say was that Lock was charged with robbing the mail!"

Mr. Gilbert handed his son some money. "Hurry up," he directed, "and overtake the packet." To Esquire Hubbard, a lawyer who chanced to be in the store, he said, "Esquire Hubbard, you go with him and see that Doty has a fair show." He then ran into the street and hailed a man passing by in a wagon. Within minutes

Augustus and Hubbard had overtaken the packet and jumped aboard at the last lock before Cumminsville. There they saw the marshall with his prisoner and learned that they were not allowed to speak to Doty. But Esquire Hubbard asserted that he was Doty's attorney and demanded the right to talk with him.

Doty told him that several days before McVicker had brought him a letter to mail. He, Doty, prepared a waybill, or routing slip, for the letter, put the two items in a wrapper marked for Rochester and threw it on a table with other letters ready for the mail bag. Later he put the letters in the bag, locked it and handed it over. After it had gone he discovered that McVicker's letter had slid under a piece of paper and been left behind. He took the old waybill out of its wrapper, made a new one dated for the next mail and stuck the first one in his pocket. The next he knew of the mattter, the marshall arrested him, found the discarded waybill in his pocket and charged him with having stolen money from the letter.

When the canalboat reached Rochester in the early evening, the marshall prepared to take Doty to jail. But Hubbard and two other Dansvillians aboard persuaded him to put the youth into their custody, guaranteeing that they would have him before the court by morning. Lockwood and Augustus stayed up all night going over and over the event, wondering what could have become of the money which Lockwood claimed he'd never seen.

When morning came at last, Hubbard and the two young men called on a noted lawyer one of them knew. He greeted them in his morning wrapper, listened to their story and gave them a note to another Rochester lawyer. "This young man is charged with robbing the mail," it read. "He is entirely inocent, and you must clear him." The three found the second lawyer at the Arcade, answered his many questions and agreed to meet him at 9 A.M. at the justice's court.

There the judge was told that McVicker's letter had come to the post office without money, that it had been opened and resealed and that the waybill from Doty's pocket as well as that of the next day were both for the same letter. McVicker, who had by then appeared on the scene, described receiving the money from Augustus Gilbert, sealing paper around it and giving it immediately to Doty to mail.

At this point an old Irish woman in the room was heard to say to a friend, "Do ye see that poor lad? Look at his face. He niver stole a cint in his life, the lamb!" Suddenly Augustus remembered that McVicker had not taken the letter directly to the post office. As he was telling this to Hubbard, he heard the judge say he would have to hold Lockwood Doty.

Sworn in, Augustus testified that McVicker had put his letter in his hat and gone to his shop, not the post office. Soon after, he came out and stood talking with a man in the street for about half an hour. During that time a boy who worked for McVicker came from his shop into the Gilberts' store, asked for a sealing wafer and returned to the shop. Questioned by the lawyer, Augustus stated that the boy had a reputation for stealing.

McVicker was then recalled and asked, "Did you hear that young man's testimony?"

"Yes, sir."

"Did he tell the truth?"

"I think he did."

"Did you take that letter from the store directly to the post office?"

"I think not. I think I was mistaken."

"When did you mail that letter?"

"I think it was the next morning when Doty was sweeping out the office."

"Where was that letter from the time you sealed it in the store until you handed it to Doty at the post office the next day?"

"In my hat."

"Where was your hat while you were across the way?"

"In the shop."

"Was it where the boy could have access to it?"

"Yes, it was on a stand in the hall of my house."

"Did the boy have access to the hall?"

"Yes, he passed through it going to his room."

"Did you know the boy had a reputation for stealing?"

"Yes."

"Did you examine that letter in the morning?"

"No, I took it from my hat and handed it to Doty."

"Did you know whether the money was in it when you handed it to Doty?"

"No, I supposed it was."

"The charge is not sustained. Case dismissed. Mr. Doty, I am happy to say you are free."

For the next few minutes Lock Doty was congratulated by one and all. The Dansvillians settled with the city lawyer, paid their hotel bill and returned home by the packet, arriving the next morning. There they found a large gathering of friends anxious to hear Doty's fate. "We did not have to declare it," Augustus Gibson wrote, concluding his tale. "They read it in our faces. And when Lockwood sprang from the deck onto the dock, a happy, free man, there was a rush to grasp his hand and express joy at his coming home without the shadow of a doubt of his entire innocence. Mr. Brown, the postmaster, made him a present of fifty dollars."

SOURCES

Bunnell, A. O., ed., *Dansville 1789-1902*
Fisher, Rosamund, *Stone Strength of the Past*

Ely S. Parker, American

As secretary to General Grant, Ely S. Parker (1828–1895), U.S. Army colonel and Seneca chief, was present when Robert E. Lee surrendered. General Lee betrayed an instant's surprise when Parker was introduced to him, but quickly regained his composure and remarked, "I am glad to see one real American here." To this the Indian replied quietly, "We are all Americans." A few minutes later the officer who was to record the terms of surrender, nervous because of the momentous occasion, spoiled several copies and turned the assignment over to Parker, who carried it out with cool efficiency.

At one time in his youth Ely worked to clear the forest for engineers preparing the extension of the Genesee Valley Canal south from Nunda to the Allegheny River. One morning when he got up, he saw fresh deer tracks out his window. He dressed, out-ran the deer, killed it and carried it back.

As these incidents point up, Ely Parker lived in two worlds. Born in 1828 on the Tonawanda Reservation, he was given both Indian and English-language names. His grandfather was a nephew of Red Jacket; when Ely was installed as a chief of the Iroquois nation, he received the medal George Washington had given Red Jacket. Although both Senecas worked to help their people, their lives formed a striking contrast. Red Jacket fought a losing battle against the tide of the white man's culture, whereas Parker became a leader in both societies.

By the age of twenty-four when he was made a sachem, taking a name meaning "He holds the door open," this youth had already lived a full life. Educated at a mission school and at Yates Academy in Orleans County, he was all of fourteen when he went as inter-preter with delegations to Albany and Washington to protest fraud in the take-over of Indian lands. Pleading for justice, he was heard respectfully by such dignitaries as Presidents Tyler and Polk.

At age sixteen Ely met Lewis Henry Morgan and began helping him in his study of Indian customs. When the anthropologist brought out *The League of the Iroquois*, the first scientific study of Indian family relations, its dedication acknowledged the author's debt to his friend. With Morgan's support, Parker attended Cayuga Academy in Aurora, later studying law in Ellicotville. But after three years of work, he was refused admission to the bar. The reason: he was neither white nor a United States citizen!

Disappointed, but not defeated, Parker determined to become an engineer. Beginning with the work at Nunda, he learned the profession on the job, studied at Rensselaer Polytechnic Institute in Troy and gradually rose to the position of first assistant engineer in the state canal office in Rochester. During his years there, he became a member of the Knights Templar of the Masons, the Atheneum and Mechanics Association and the New York Militia. Meanwhile he continued to represent Indians in defense of their land. One of his achievements was to negotiate the treaty by which the government gave up its attempt to move the Tonawanda Indians to Kansas and allowed them to own their reservation.

After several other engineering jobs, Parker was appointed to one in Galena, Illinois, where he became a good friend of Ulysses S. Grant. With the outbreak of the Civil War, Parker applied for a commission—again to be refused on account of his race. It took two years before Grant could succeed in having Parker assigned to his staff. The next year Parker became a lieutenant-colonel and the general's military secretary.

After the war Parker continued to work for Grant and was commissioned brigadier general in recognition of gallant and meritorious services. General Grant gave the bride away when Parker married Minnie Sackett Wast, a pretty Washington socialite. One of President Grant's first appointments was to make his old friend Commissioner of Indian Affairs, the first of his race to win that position. Grant originated what was for the time a humane and just policy of educating and protecting the Indians, which Parker carried out capably.

His fairness earned him enemies, however, and persons who

had previously profited from graft tried to oust him by accusing him of mishandling federal money. Although all charges were proved false, Parker was disillusioned about political life and resigned. For some years he made profitable business investments, then later lost a fortune. He was superintendent for buildings and supplies of the New York City Police Department when he died in 1895.

Before he was born, Parker's mother had dreamed that she would have a son who would become "a white man as well as an Indian" and that "His sun will rise on Indian land and set on the white man's land. Yet the land of his ancestors will fold him in death." Ely Parker's body had been buried in Connecticut, but it was later removed to Forest Lawn Cemetery in Buffalo near the graves of other Senecas, Red Jacket among them. And so the prophecy was fulfilled.

SOURCES

Armstrong, William H., *Warrior in Two Camps: Ely S. Parker*
Dockstader, Frederick J., *Great North American Indians*

Poet John H. McNaughton

When John Hugh McNaughton (1829–1891) died, his obituary writer said he had written of the Genesee Valley as Sir Walter Scott had written of Scotland and as Washington Irving had of the Hudson Valley. The comparison was apt. Like Scott, he was Scottish, the son of pioneers who named their new home in northwestern Livingston County Caledonia, the Latin name for Scotland. Like Irving, he celebrated the charm of his part of New York State and spun romances of its history.

John Hugh McNaughton attended Temple Hill Academy in Geneseo and the Academy at Riga where he began to write poems and set them to music. Later he contributed articles on musicology to scholarly journals. He then turned to writing sheet music, or "parlor music," as it was called. He was very successful at this: five of his songs sold 450,000 copies each.

They were of the "hearts and flowers" type so popular in the Civil War era. Among them were "Faded Coat of Blue" about a soldier, "Sweet Belle Mahone" addressed to a girl who had died, and its companion, "Jamie True," which included Belle's response,

> "Gazing down from heaven's gate
> where I longing, lingering wait,
> Watch I'm keeping over you,
> Jamie, Jamie true."

The poet named a volume of verse for his farm on the Caledonia-Avon road, *Babble Brook Songs*. Henry Wadsworth Longfellow wrote of them, "Your poems have touched me very much. Tears fell down my cheeks as I read them." His poem, "Red Jacket," was read at the celebration of the centennial of the

126

founding of Geneseo in 1890. In it the Seneca chief returns from the dead to chastise white men for their greed and hypocrisy.

"Poet John's" major work is *Onnalinda*. This book-length poem tells of an Iroquois princess who outwits a French general in his attack on her father's territory and whose beauty wins the heart of a young French captain. British audiences were ahead of Americans in acclaiming this work. One way of publishing a book at that time was to show prospective buyers the manuscript and secure subscriptions, or promises of purchase, in enough numbers to underwrite the cost of producing the book. Accordingly, McNaughton's son-in-law, William Byam, went to England with letters of introduction to members of the nobility. Fortunate in securing the subscriptions of two princesses, he was able to add the names of 341 peers within ten months. He then hired canvassers who obtained 4,000 more subscribers at a rate of from five to ten dollars each.

After the English edition of *Onnalinda* was underway, Byam made arrangements for the American editions. He hired artists to make steel engravings for the illustated versions. (A French artist, by the way, showed the Indian maiden wearing a bustle and shoes with French heels!) The de-luxe copy of the book was bound in mauve silk, another in white leather with gold lettering. The poem went to eight editions and sold more than 40,000 copies.

Fashions in literature change, and *Onnalinda*'s popularity has waned. But John Hugh McNaughton's poem lived in another way—his great, great granddaughter was named Onnalinda.

SOURCE

Biographical Review, The Leading Citizens of Livingston and Wyoming Counties

By Deeds of Healing: The Career of Cordelia Greene, M.D.

"Why can't I be a doctor, too?" nineteen-year-old Cordelia Greene (1831–1905) asked her father. The year was 1850, and she had read a newspaper account of Elizabeth Blackwell's receiving her medical degree. Jabez Greene was proprietor of The Water Cure in the Western New York hamlet of Castile, a sanitarium conducted according to hydropathy, a method of treating disease by use of water. He knew that his daughter had special aptitude for caring for the sick.

"There's no reason why you can't," he replied, but added, "It may be pleasant to study medicine, but it is quite another thing to practice it." This was but the first of many ambivalent viewpoints Cordelia was to encounter in her career as a physician. Threading her way through a maze of trends, counter-trends, paradoxes and contradictions, she side-stepped the difficulties encountered by many women doctors of the first generation to enjoy a long, successful and trouble-free practice. How did she do it?

The stigma then attached to a woman's becoming a physician was indeed formidable. Elizabeth Blackwell had been admitted to Geneva (N.Y.) Medical College only because the faculty, loath to offend the physician who had recommended her, put the matter to a vote by the students. Most of them thought it a joke and voted to admit her. Two years after Elizabeth had graduated with honor, this same school refused the application of her sister Emily. When in 1850 Harriot Hunt tried for the second time to attend Harvard College medical lectures, the faculty first granted permission, then gave in to student protests and withdrew it. The Female Medical College of Pennsylvania's first graduation ceremony in 1851 was nearly interrupted by 500 rioting male students. Newspapers

128

poked fun at "doctresses," one calling them "hens that want to be cocks."

Yet Cordelia knew, from helping in her father's sanitarium, that she had a gift for healing. She must have known, too, that caring for the sick has from ancient times been a traditional role of women, allied as it is to the nurture of children. And, though it was no longer acceptable among the urban-educated for women to be midwives, midwifery was still practiced in rural areas, and people no doubt recalled that some of them had been skilled practitioners.

Young Cordelia wanted a career, but after a year's experience she had at age 19 given up teaching, the one profession then fully open to women. To her mind, medicine was not a preposterous goal. As the historian Mary Walsh has observed, "If women were to enter any profession, their 'special' talent for nurturing seemed to indicate a career in medicine. . . . Certainly it was easier in the nineteenth century to envision a woman pursuing a career at someone's bedside than in a courtroom, brokerage house or political club."

Still, it was the prevailing opinion that women's intellects were too limited for medical training and their physical strength unequal to its demands. Women needed protection from the unpleasant realities of the world outside their ordained sphere of home and family. Granted that young ladies might pursue higher education, society dictated that only certain subjects were suitable for them. The study of the male anatomy was decidedly not one of them. What would follow upon a female's loss of her modesty but the erosion of her purity?

This view was not limited to men. As late as until 1869 the Female Medical College of Pennsylvania would hold to its policy that

> in all special diseases of men and women and in all operations necessarily involving embarrassing exposure of the person, it is neither fitting nor expedient that both sexes should attend promiscuously; but that all special diseases of men should be treated by men in the presence of men only.

On the other hand, "A new generation of women is on the stage," Lucretia Mott proclaimed. "Mind has no sex," she told a group of male medical students. Female seminaries had proliferated since their founding in the 1830's, and it was no longer unusual for a girl to aim for higher education. A number of forces were challenging the old stereotypes. Upstate New York was the breeding-ground for reforms of every sort, from socialistic and religious communities to temperance and abolitionism. Cordelia's sympathy with the feminist movement, which had been founded twelve years before in nearby Seneca Falls, was in harmony with her Quaker heritage. One of her forebears had been persecuted for her faith in seventeenth-century New England and later became the heroine of a poem by John Greenleaf Whittier. A Quaker grandmother who lived with the family may well have influenced her in favor of this cause. When she was eighteen Cordelia had a conversion experience which led her to join the Presbyterian Church and to determine to devote her life to the service of others.

Against this background of contradictory forces, Miss Greene enrolled in the fifth session of the Female Medical College in Philadelphia in 1854. The four-year delay was presumably due to her need to save up tuition money. In Philadelphia she earned living expenses by housecleaning and caring for the sick. She attended only one five-month session, which lasted into March 1855. One reason she did not complete her studies at Female Medical College may have been its lack of clinical instruction, as Dr. Ann Preston had not yet established the Woman's Hospital to provide the opportunity for bedside teaching. As the fledgling college continued to graduate women, opposition from the medical fraternity mounted. Within a few years the Philadelphia Medical Society would formalize its hostility to the college by passing "resolutions of communication against every physician who should teach in [it] and every woman who graduated from it and everybody else who would consult with such teachers."

Whether or not these were the causes, Miss Greene transferred to Cleveland Medical College (later part of Western Reserve University), again working to pay expenses. There she joined Marie Zakrzewska, destined to help Elizabeth Blackwell establish New York Infirmary for Women and Children and to found New England Hospital for Women and Children. With two other women, Cordelia and Marie made a foursome among several hundred men students.

This experience was both discouraging and heartening.

Zakrzewska later summed it up by saying, "The young men did not like our presence; some of the professors acted as if we did not exist; and others favored us in many ways." Although other boarders where she took her meals would leave when she and her roommate entered the room, she wrote of "trotting unconcernedly to and from the college past neighbors staring from behind half-shut blinds." There, she reported, "We four women had our box seat to ourselves, unmolested by the tobacco-chewing and spitting Aesculapians in embryo." When these men had petitioned to have women excluded in the coming term, the faculty refused, having promised the four their chance of graduating. But, they assured the gentlemen, they would admit no new women students in the future. Perhaps Dr. Harriot Hunt was not aware of this decision when she visited the college, for she was favorably impressed, writing, "Men and women studying together at a medical college of high standing was prophetic."

There is significance to Cordelia Greene's career in Dr. Hunt's phrase, "a medical college of high standing." This was a time of low standards in medicine; the American Medical Association had recently been formed because of the need to upgrade medical education. Most medical colleges were proprietary institutions, i.e., operated at a profit by individuals, from which the most mediocre scholar could be graduated after a mere two terms of lectures. Several years hence Elizabeth Blackwell would say of the estimated 300 women who had by then graduated from "some semblance" of a medical course, "It is not until they leave college and attempt their work alone and unaided that they realize how utterly insufficient their education is. . . . A few gain a little practical knowledge and struggle into a second rate position."

The wish of many male doctors to raise the standard of medicine—to professionalize it—was one reason for their antipathy to women in the field. Since the early 1800's the establishment had barred women from practicing midwifery, not only because of their lack of formal training, but also because some of them engaged in abortion. By extension, women physicians were also suspect. The men objected as well to a certain few women entrants into their ranks who were not deeply committed to medicine but had gone into the field as a means of broadening women's rights. (Blackwell herself was one by her own admission, as was that true Upstate New York eccentric, Dr. Mary Walker.) Women also posed the threat of increased competition for patients and for places in medical schools.

Moreover, "regular" medicine was being challenged by numerous competing schools of thought. Chief of these was homeopathy, which, operating in the belief that "like cures like," advocated drugs in minute quantities to produce reactions like the patient's symptoms. Allopathy, the orthodox theory, used methods to produce effects opposite of illness. A third group, the eclectics, combined methods of the first two. Another was the Thomsonians, or Botanics, who expressed their faith in nature's curative powers by prescribing only vegetable compounds. Hydropathy, as exemplified in Jabez Greene's Water Cure, was still widely popular, while rivalling these were the claims of magnetists, clairvoyants, phrenologists and mesmerists. With the doors of traditional medical schools so hard for women to open, it is no wonder that many of them attended proprietary schools run by adherents of one or another of these viewpoints, who were eager to accept any disciples.

Cordelia Greene could not be criticized on any of these grounds. Her M.D. was from a reputable college where she had received the same education as the men students, including clinical experience. She was graduated with honors, her thesis rated at the time as "one of the best ever presented." Cleveland Medical College was in the allopathic camp, and as Walsh has observed, "Although the line between irregular and regular medicine for most of the nineteenth century was a spurious one with neither side holding a monopoly on scientific truth, in retrospect, the future clearly lay with the regulars."

Yet, armed as she was with credentials beyond reproach, Dr. Greene chose to ally herself with the proponents of hydropathy. After working two years in her father's establishment, she spent six years on the staff of the Clifton Springs (N.Y.) Sanitarium. Besides the power of its sulphur springs, this hydropathic institute featured a strong spiritual atmosphere as a curative force. Highly praised by her associates, Dr. Greene was said to have done much to build the sanitarium's patronage. When her father died in 1864, she acted on her brothers' suggestion that she buy his Water Cure and continue her work in Castile. With this she "covered both bases," laying the groundwork for her successful career.

Hydropathy was part of what has been variously named the popular health and health reform movements. It is best understood against the background of the state of orthodox medicine at the time. In hindsight this can only be termed appalling. Antisepsis was still in the future; disease was thought to emanate from unwholesome environments, such as night fogs or miasmas generated from improperly filled land. Thermometers and stethoscopes were unknowns.

Dr. Oliver Wendell Holmes was ridiculed by his colleagues for suggesting that septic poisoning of women in childbirth was due to the unclean hands of physicians. As Rhoda Truax has reported, "Most surgeons washed their hands after they finished operating, rather than before or between operations. Most of them wore old frock coats put aside for the purpose and thrown away when they became too encrusted with blood and filth to be of further use—the state of a surgeon's coat was often regarded as an index of how busy and successful he was." A professor of medicine in 1858 advocated inserting leeches into women's wombs even though he knew this caused intense suffering.

"Bleeding, purging and puking, the unholy trinity," a doctor of a later generation termed the popular remedies of this era. According to the scholar, Regina Morantz, "Medical treatment usually consisted of massive doses of extremely dangerous substances—mercury, lead, calomel and opium. Heavy bleeding with the lancet proved all too popular. Physicians often cauterized the cervical area by the use of hot irons or silver nitrate solution in order to treat venereal disease, as well as a host of lesser female complaints." It is estimated that the average patient of the time had little more than a fifty-fifty chance of benefiting from an encounter with the average doctor. A half-serious attack on orthodox practice claimed, "No matter what the sickness, the patient is first bled; secondly an emetic is given; thirdly a potion of calomel, to be followed with salts and jallops, and usually a blister plaster is applied to some parts of the body."

Furthermore, poor health habits such as excessive food and drink, unventilated rooms and little exercise were the general rule. "I am not able to recall in my immense circle of friends and acquaintances all over the Union so many as *ten* married ladies born in this century and country who are perfectly sound, healthy and vigorous," wrote Catharine Beecher. Another problem was the reluctance of many women to be treated by males for reasons of modesty. Harriot Hunt had summed up the situation back in 1830 when, writing of the treatment of her sister's illness by male physicians, she reported, "After forty-one weeks of sickness and one hundred professional calls . . . , we came to the conclusion that her case was not understood." She explained their alliance with irregular practitioners, saying, "It did not occur to us that to die under regular practice and with medical etiquette was better than any other way."

Into this vacuum came one lay evangelist after another, each proclaiming a special nostrum. They advocated, singly or in combination, dietary reform, loose clothing, hypnosis, spiritualism, temperance, hygiene and the water cure.

Originated by Vincent Priessnitz, a Silesian farmer, hydropathy was first introduced in America by Henry Gardiner Wright when Bronson Alcott persuaded him to bring the doctrine here from England. As popularized by the Rev. Sylvester Graham, an evangelist and temperance lecturer. In the belief that water is a natural life-sustaining element, hydropathists advocated it "internally, externally and eternally." Between 1823 and 1900, 213 water cure sanitariums were founded in which people could avail themselves of steam baths, plunge baths, douche baths, sitz baths, wet compresses, wet girdles, wet wrappings, wet sheet packs and sweating cradles. Such luminaries as Catharine Beecher, Harriet Beecher Stowe, Julia Ward Howe, Horace Greeley and Henry Wadsworth Longfellow espoused this regimen.

Practitioners of hydropathy also took part in other reforms, such as endorsing exercise, temperance, anti-tobacco and "anti-lacing" in place of the fashionable corsets which deformed women's ribs. An interest in female hygiene and sex education was another characteristic. Ladies' Physiological Reform Societies were organized to dispel women's mistification about their bodies.

Cordelia Greene had personal reasons for subscribing to the tenets of hydropathy. In the year before she enrolled at Female Medical College she had had what was then called "lung trouble" or "consumption." Chronically depressed and fearful of death, she is said to have revived and begun improving when her father told her, "If you are going to die, I wish you would go down to the grave cheerfully!" In fact, his treatment did cure her. Again, during her tenure at Clifton Springs Sanitarium, she nearly died from blood poisoning after conducting a post-mortem examination and attributed a miraculous recovery to the spiritual atmosphere of the Sanitarium.

Nor was her training at Female Medical College entirely at odds with the hydropathic emphasis on preventive medicine and treating the whole person. Dr. Ann Preston, Cordelia's physiology professor in 1854, took the remarkably advanced view that "there is not a disorder, from a scratch on the toe to an inflammation of the brain that may not be modified by mental emotion." Reflecting Ambrose Pare's injunction, "First, do no harm," she taught that "pure air, proper diet, well-regulated exercise, the right government of passions come first in the catalogue of healing, and preserving agencies and 'medicines' . . . are always subsidiaries." Ann Jackson Wood points out that most of the first generation of women doctors chose hygiene, or preventive medicine, as their special emphasis.

Finally, the aim of hydropathic practitioners to teach women how their bodies function dovetailed with those of the burgeoning feminist movement. Efforts to improve the health of women and women's rights in general became intertwined.

For Cordelia Greene these considerations were subsumed under the fact that her father's practice and the facilities of the Castile Water Cure were hers for the taking. It seems safe to assume that she was inspired by the spirit of Ann Preston's injunction, "Your business is not to war with words, but to make good your position upon the bodies of your patients by deeds of healing."

In the 1860's the difficulties of women medical students, great as they were, were fewer than those they met in establishing a practice. Dr. Zakrzewska had found, as she later reported, that women M.D.'s were social outcasts and that no respectable family would let rooms to a woman doctor. Cordelia Greene's experience was the opposite. When her brothers suggested that she buy her father's sanitarium, she was strengthened in her decision by the welcome given her by various townspeople. "You had better come home," they assured her. A Castile judge asked, "Why don't you come here and live with us? We will do all we can to make a success of the enterprise."

Popular belief would have it that rural areas lag behind cities in adjusting to new notions, but here the reverse was true. Evidently the fact that the villagers had known Cordelia all her life and thought of her as one of them made the difference. No doubt the presence of a woman doctor offended Victorian sensibilities less when it became apparent that the doctor would treat only women. Also, Castilians were soon grateful for the prestige and prosperity which the water cure brought to the village, whose only industries up to then had been a grist mill, a saw mill and thirteen distilleries.

"Dr. Cordelia," as she was often called opened the Castile Sanitarium with one patient. Its later success must be attributed to her remarkable ability and personal qualities. The Sanitarium building, twice enlarged, accommodated thirty-three patients, with some thirty more boarded nearby, and the facilities were always used to capacity. Although it was never advertised, the Sanitarium attracted patients from every part of the country and from abroad. Rose Cleveland, sister of the President, described Dr. Greene in *Century* magazine as one of the foremost woman physicians in America. She became in time a member of the Wyoming County, New York State and American Medical Associations, and the county group often met at her sanitarium.

Soon after opening her establishment, Dr. Greene hired as an assistant Clara Swain, a young Castile woman. Swain later graduated from Female Medical College, was America's first woman medical graduate to go as a missionary to the Orient and became director of India's first hospital for women. Three other women doctors successively assisted Dr. Greene: Drs. Caroline Stevens, Mary I. Slade and Jessica W. Findlay. They were followed by her niece, Dr. Mary Greene, who eventually became proprietor of the sanitarium. In addition Dr. Greene supervised the work of several nurses, a cook, housekeeper, gardener, business assistant and maintenance workers. As if this did not give full scope to her talents, she adopted six children, four of whom grew up together and were devoted to her.

Her diagnostic ability was perhaps the doctor's outstanding trait. So quick was she to discover a patient's basic trouble that some of them believed she was clairvoyant. Even discounting the fervent praise of many awe-struck, doting women, there is adequate testimony that a number of Greene's patients had been treated without success by noted physicians here and in Europe before she cured them. It seems clear that she had strong intuition—what Jerome Bruner has called "knowing with the left hand."

Dr. Greene would have said that this ability was rooted in her cooperating with God's will in bringing a person to full health. She unabashedly proclaimed her faith and encouraged it in others as an important part of their recovery. Every morning saw her leading family prayers with her staff and every evening a prayer service for patients in the parlor. She prayed aloud for her patients, often imploring them to do the same. Many are the reports of her repeated sayings: "Holiness is simply wholeness," "In quietness and confidence shall be your strength," "Trust in the Lord and do good; breathe deeply and eat good food" and "Help us to learn to say, 'It is all right.'"

Allied to this positive thinking was her belief in controlled breathing as a therapy. "Breathe deeply; all the air belongs to us, but we can have only as much as we will breathe in." "Forage for air. Breathe through the nose as if smelling a rose at a little distance." These and similar injunctions she rehearsed repeatedly.

Unlike some of the water cures which mushroomed throughout the eastern United States, the Castile Sanitarium was no resort hotel. The most famous of those catering to both men and women, Wesselhoeft's Water-Cure Establishment in Brattleboro, Vt., offered guests the use of a bowling alley, billiards room and gymnasium. The diarist George Templeton Strong satirized it as "combining usages appropriate to a German watering-place, an insane asylum and a penitentiary." A few miles away from Castile in Dansville was Dr. James C. Jackson's water cure, Our Home on the Hill, which encouraged such amenities as card playing and weekly dances. Recreational equipment at Dr. Greene's establishment was limited to India rubber balls, bean bags, "grace hoops" and a melodion for hymn-sings.

Tolerating no nonsense, Dr. Cordelia enforced the rigors of hydropathy. Every morning at six each patient was either doused with a pail of cold water, followed by one of warm water, or had a cold dripping sheet thrown over her. A full glass of water had to be drunk before breakfast, and the doctor would call at the room of any recalcitrants. A spare diet was an important part of the treatment. Fatty meats, starches, spices and coffee were outlawed and wheat, milk, eggs, fish, fruit and vegetables featured. Dr.

Greene found time to write *The Art of Keeping Well* and *The Castile Sanitarium Cook Book* to promote her theories of nutrition. Eating between meals was strictly forbidden, as she thought her own chronic depression as a young girl had been partly caused by an enlarged liver and poor circulation through the head due to her having eaten between meals.

Exercise and outdoor life were stressed in the sanitarium's program, with Cordelia Greene a persuasive example. She exercised regularly before breakfast and at bedtime and did gymnastics into her seventies. Often working fifteen hours a day, she had unusual stamina and endurance.

Predictably, she was a staunch temperance advocate. Here her efforts extended beyond her institution to the community. For many years she paid for notices inserted in the Castile paper such as:

> An ounce a day or the occasional use of the purest whiskey, brandy, wine or beer will fix upon the brain the alcohol appetite. This habit:
> > Dulls the conscience,
> > Intensifies the passions,
> > Destroys self-control,
> > Perverts physical perception,
> > Distorts moral vision.

When a fireman's convention brought beer into the town, she learned where it was hidden and had the door locked, conveniently losing the key. She then recruited and chaperoned a group of girls who served the men lemonade.

Not only could "Dr. Cordelia" make her patients walk miles in bitter weather, do calisthenics and forego sweets, she made them like it—and her. A saving sense of humor seems to have lain beneath her Puritanism. With charm and tact she cajoled her charges into obeying her spartan dictates. Abounding in cheeriness, she had a fund of sayings to combat difficulties. "No indeed," she assured patients who feared they had cancer, "there isn't enough to go around." She was fond of saying, "Any fool can lie down and die, but it takes a brave woman to live." She set the tone for such customs as creeping races, charades and play-readings and inspired the Sanitarium yell, which began, "Breathe—stretch—

breathe" and ended "C - U - R - E - D, Hurrah! Hurrah! Hurrah!, Hurrah for Doctor Greene!"

Such naive revelry was a surface expression of the supportive community that Dr. Greene's sanitarium was for many women. In this sisterhood they enjoyed the freedom of being able to discuss their physical and emotional problems. A shared fellowship was a definite element in the water cure's therapy. This was intensified as Dr. Greene worked for the cause of woman's suffrage and made friends among leaders of the movement. Susan B. Anthony, Frances Willard and Rev. Anna Howard Shaw were among those who came to her for recuperation from their work. As Castile's largest taxpayer, she once informed its Town Board, "Gentlemen, taxation without representation is tyranny," and she noted ironically that the mentally-retarded uncle whom she cared for could vote, when she could not.

When asked what she would want as the form of a testimonial from patients, she chose a free library for Castile and donated money and land for it. The fiftieth anniversary of her residence in Castile was celebrated in 1899 by several hundred friends, neighbors and former patients. Her classmate, Dr. Marie Zakrzewska of New England Hospital for Women and Children sent a greeting saying it should become the custom to honor single women on the fiftieth anniversary of their being wedded to their professions. "I feel that the spirit of a girl of sixteen is inside of me," Dr. Greene declared at age sixty-eight. "I like to work and I like almost everything except quarreling and fighting—yes, and I like to fight when there is a principle involved."

Besides the library which bears her name, Cordelia Greene, M.D. left a legacy in her part in the health reform movement. The practitioners of hydropathy deserve some of the credit for the current concern with hygiene, healthful nutrition and fitness and for the growing demand among women to understand and control their own bodies.

SOURCES

Alsop, Gulielma F., *History of the Woman's Medical College, Philadelphia, Penn. 1850-1950*

Branch, Edward, *The Sentimental Years, 1830-1860*

The Castilian, Sept. 12, 1902

Chaff, Sandra L., Letter to author

Ehrenreich, Barbara and Deirdre English, *Witches, Midwives and Nurses:*
   A History of Women Healers

Gordon, Elizabeth, *Story of the Life and Work of Cordelia Greene, M.D.*

Morantz, Regina, In *Clio's Consciousness Raised*

Marion, John F., *Philadelphia Medica*

Shryock, Richard H., *Medicine in America: Historical Essays*

Sklar, Kathryn Kish, "All Hail to Pure Cold Water!"

————, *Catharine Beecher: A Study in American Domesticity*

Strong, George Templeton, Diary

Taussig, Ellen, *Buffalo Evening News Magazine*

Tomlinson, George B., *From Youth to Seventy*

Traux, Rhoda, *The Doctors Warren of Boston, First Family of Surgery*

Vietor, Agnes, ed., *A Woman's Quest: The Life of Marie A. Zakrsewska*

Walsh, Mary R., *Doctors Wanted: No Women Need Apply*

Wood, Ann Douglas In *Clio's Consciousness Raised*

Zakrzewska, Marie A., "Fifty Years Ago—A Retrospect"

Henry Ward, Naturalist and Explorer

A born naturalist, Henry Ward (1834–1906) began collecting specimens at the age of three when he found and treasured a pebble of the rare stone, gneiss hornblende. As he went on to make Ward's Natural Science Establishment known to scientists the world over, he led a fascinated—and fascinating—life.

When his first find occurred, Henry lived next door to his grandfather, Dr. Levi Ward, Rochester businessman and philanthropist. At age ten he went on geological excursions along the Genesee conducted by Dr. Chester Dewey, principal of Rochester High School. Once wanting Dr. Dewey to identify a fossil, young Henry found him about to preside at high school commencement exercises and walked up to him on a platform, having to be told to ask his question another time. This did not in the least diminish the boy's interest in geology and collecting.

When he was twelve, Henry took the first of the many trips that would later dominate his life. After his father deserted his family to find greater opportunities in Chicago, Henry set off alone to join him and, with the help of a stranger, found him. But Henry's family had to be told where he was, and a clerk from his grandfather's office took an unrepentant adventurer back to Rochester.

Henry was then sent to Moscow (Leicester) to work on the farm of Jeredia Horsford in return for his keep and the chance to attend the district school. After that this fifteen-year-old began two years' study at Middlebury Academy in Wyoming, New York, supporting himself almost entirely by doing janitorial work and carpentry as well as digging and cleaning wells. Impressed by his determination, Henry's uncle, Levi A. Ward, proposed that he put him through Williams College in Massachusetts. But the youth was not adequately prepared to do well in any study except his beloved geology, and when the family would not allow him to join a professor's geological expedition, he left college.

Now considered a failure, Henry worked in his Uncle Levi's insurance office and attended N. W. Benedict's Academy in Rochester, to be recalled later by a schoolmate as "rather a rough specimen of humanity . . . (whose) chief interests were in rocks, fossils and shells." Two weeks of reading law in the office of his uncle, Judge Samuel Selden, convinced him that this was not the profession for him.

Then a third uncle came to his rescue—the Rev. Ferdinand Ward, pastor of the Presbyterian Church in Geneseo, understanding Henry's wish to be a geologist, offered to pay his way through Geneseo's Temple Hill Academy. A sympathetic principal there gave this student the paid work of labeling and arranging a rock collection which had been given to the school by James S. Wadsworth. When General Wadsworth's son, Charles, an Academy student, caught Henry's enthusiasm for geology, the General financed a collecting trip which the two young men took to northern New York State as well as one which Ward and a friend took to Nova Scotia. Another friendship which Henry Ward made that year was with Phebe Howell, an Academy student from York, who he said was "a most perfect chemist and geologist."

Back at Temple Hill, Ward was teaching the Primary Department when a letter from the Albany geologist, James Hall, asked him to deliver a greeting to Louis Agassiz when the famous naturalist came to lecture in Rochester. Since he could not afford a carriage, Ward walked to the city. After the lecture he was delegated to show the celebrity Rochester's geological points of interest, and the pair spent a happy day exploring rock formations of the Rochester Lower Falls and the Pinnacle hills.

The next day Agassiz met with the Ward family to announce that he would take on their difficult youth as his assistant in his Museum of Comparative Zoology if they would underwrite the remaining cost of his three years at Harvard. To their credit, they agreed, and Henry spent little time on farewells as he headed for Cambridge.

Though it was an important influence on his career, Ward's work with Agassiz had lasted less then a year when fortune favored him once again. General Wadsworth would pay his expenses if he would be a companion to Charles and study with him at the great Paris School of Mines. Soon after they reached Paris, however, Charles became ill, and the General sent them on a tour to the milder climate of Egypt and Palestine. Quite unlike the conventional sightseeing which Wadsworth had envisioned, the young men's travels took them 1,100 miles up the Nile, included some enjoyable adventures and, of course, added considerably to their geologic collections. In Paris again in 1855, Ward was significantly influenced by the Paris Exposition as a means of educating people in science's discoveries.

When the price of Genesee Valley wheat declined the next year, as did General Wadsworth's generosity, Charles was summoned home and Ward left penniless. But fossils saved the day— they were important to scientists at this time when controversy raged over Darwin's theory of evolution. Ward got permission from Madame Cliquot, owner of a famous winery, in France to collect fossils from her limestone-walled wine cellars. He took trunks of these to sell to the British Museum, collected fossils in England and sold them to the Imperial Museum in Paris.

In this way he financed a trip through Central Europe and back to Paris via Venice and another to Russia, Scandinavia and Holland, while at the same time making his acquaintance with museum directors and scientists. Meanwhile, too, he shipped hundreds of pounds of specimens for his own and the Wadsworths' "cabinets," or collections, for which Uncle Levi and the General uncomplainingly paid the considerable express charges.

In 1858 and '59 Ward extended his collecting trips with a new motive: he would send specimens home to help educate the American public in natural history. He spent every penny his sales brought him on more samples, lived on a mere subsistence and several times was so short of cash he slept under an arch of the London Bridge. After a balloon flight in France and a trip to Spain and Portugal, Ward was forced to return home, and, with a view to seeing all that he could en route, sailed westward—but only to the Canary Islands.

There he could not resist the lure of traveling for little money as a deck passenger to Fernando Po, an island off the west coast of Africa. Then on a voyage up the Niger River, he became very ill with Blackwater fever, so ill that the captain of the boat which took him back to Fernando Po, fearing contagion, put him ashore to die. Miraculously, a native woman who was a Christian convert and who could speak a little French, nursed him back to health. (Ward, who characterized himself as a "Christian agnostic," later sent her a box of gifts including a French-language Bible.) Eventually he reached Havana and, by a roundabout route, Rochester.

Ward now renewed his determination to make his own collection a means of scientific education, even though this would require still further purchases to fill in gaps. Rising to the occasion as before, Uncle Levi offered the necessary funds with the expectation that it would later be sold at a profit. Henry Ward was off again to Europe. This time, instead of going to the wilds in search of items, he bought them, and his only excitement was discussing Africa with the explorer, David Livingstone, at a formal reception in London.

A professorship, at the University of Rochester, which had been offered him for sometime, began in 1860, and that year Phebe Howell and Henry Ward were married. For a while it seemed that he had settled down. Some 40,000 specimens in 170 crates had to be moved to a hired hall and classes taught in zoology and botany as well as geology. He tried to sell his cabinet for $23,000, but the outbreak of the Civil War diverted interest in it. Then the trustees of the University of Rochester agreed to house it if it were given to the University, and, reducing the price to $20,000, Ward began to raise the money by individual subscriptions. He sold a smaller collection to Vassar Female Seminary (later College) but lost money on the transaction. Undaunted, Ward dreamed of building a three-part collection which would teach zoology and botany as well as geology and wrote to a friend:

> I have a determination of the most stubborn, unrelenting, dog-
> ged kind to reach the end which I am aiming at . . . I have the
> whale, porpoise, hippopotamus, elephant . . .

The list continues with thirty more specimens, ending with a triumphant "and GORILLA!" This last was the object of great, if disturbing, curiosity to Rochesterians because of Darwin's thories. It was later sold to Vassar where for years it was provided with a pair of shorts!

To house his zoological collection, Ward built a workshop on the campus which he named Cosmos Hall and later put up Chronos Hall next door for his casts of fossils and many duplicates of all sorts. When his sales of subscriptions eventually reached their goal, he moved the geological cabinet to Anderson Hall. By then later additions had made the collection worth more than the $20,000 he received, but this perfectionist was more interested in science than profit.

A new enthusiasm claimed him in 1865 when several Rochester investors hired him to develop gold properties in Montana. Ward operated a mine successfully, but when it ran out and his backers refused to invest more capital, lost his share of the investment. Meanwhile he had enjoyed two years of roughing it in the West. On another leave from his university teaching, he developed a gold-mining operation in North Carolina for Cyrus McCormick, but this, too, ended in failure.

A far more devastating event was the fire which destroyed both Cosmos and Chronos Halls in 1869. Aside from the set-back to his scholarly pursuits, the financial loss was tremendous: only $5,000-worth of the collection valued at $68,000 was saved. Ward's only possible response was to begin again; five days later he erected a building across the road from the campus. This was the official start of Ward's Natural Science Establishment as a commercial venture separate from the University. Over the gateway leading to it, Ward erected the lower jaw of a whale as an arch. A sign at the entrance proclaimed, "This is not a museum, but a working establishment where all are very busy." Ward had by then attracted to his work a number of able young men, some of whom were to go on to important positions in the natural sciences. They were indeed busy as orders for specimens and casts poured in from museums and schools throughout the country and abroad. Ward gave up teaching that year and went to Europe to replenish his losses from the fire.

The next years were a time of even more travel. Ward went on a buffalo hunt with the Grand Duke of Russia and Buffalo Bill Cody. He assembled a collection for the University of Virginia and built exhibits for the Chicago Exposition and the Centennial Exposition in Philadelphia. Buying trips took him to Europe three times, to Egypt and to British Guiana. From Germany he brought back a stuffed mammoth sixteen feet high and twenty-six feet long, a popular sensation. In the 1880's he visited Australia, New Zealand, Singapore, Borneo and Siam, went down the east coast of Africa and toured Mexico. In all, he crossed the Atlantic more than fifty times. When P. T. Barnum's gigantic elephant, Jumbo, had a losing encounter with a locomotive, Ward was commissioned to mount his skin and bones.

In the early 1880's Henry Ward was seized by a new passion: meteorites. His search for them took him the length of South America and to Mexico and Australia again. Phebe Ward died in 1891, and six years later Ward married Lydia Avery Coonley, a wealthy widow originally from Wyoming, New York.

Mrs. Coonley-Ward, as she called herself, generously funded her husband's searches for meteorites, and wherever one fell there Ward hurried, his adventures worthy of inclusion in "The Arabian Nights." He was planning a trip to the Andes when on a visit to Buffalo, he was run over and killed by an automobile—an ironic fate for one who had traveled to so many dangerous and exotic places. His gravestone in Rochester's Mt. Hope cemetery is what he had found and chosen for the purpose, a huge glacial boulder of jasper conglomerate.

The many risks which Henry Ward took were never for the sake of adventure in itself but for his goal of teaching natural history to the people. He revolutionized the world's museums, changing them from simple collections of specimens into displays of representative forms which taught the process of evolution. Moreover, he left a legacy in the many scientists he trained. His life was cut short abruptly, but it had been full enough for several ordinary people.

SOURCES

Fairchild, H. L., *Henry Augustus Ward*
Jensen, David, "A Business Started with a Pebble"
Katz, Herbert and Marjorie, *Museums, U.S.A.*
Strong, Augustus H., *Henry A. Ward: Reminiscence and Appreciation*
The University of Rochester: The First One Hundred Years 1850-1950
"Ward, Henry", *Dictionary of American Biography*
Ward, Roswell, *Henry A. Ward: Museum Builder to America*

The Shakers at Sonyea

Two places in the Valley, Sodus on Lake Ontario and Sonyea in Groveland, have been home to communities of the Society of Believers in Christ's Second Appearing—or, as others call them, the Shakers. Founded by Mother Ann Lee in England in the 1760's, the Society came to America in 1774. Since they had split off from the Quakers, its members were first termed Shaking Quakers, then Shakers, because of their practice of whirling, trembling and shaking during worship, which they believed rid them of sin. Convinced that sexual activity even within marriage was sinful and expecting the imminent end of this world, they were celibate. They renounced all that they considered worldly to form colonies in which all property was held in common; they believed in strictly segregating the sexes; and they gave women equal authority with men.

"Work as though you had a thousand years to live and as you would if you knew you must die tomorrow" was a Shaker maxim. With a schedule of work from five in the morning to eight at night, the communes were often models of efficiency. Primarily agricultural, they included many other trades, soon becoming largely self-sufficient. Shakers were the first in this country to import registered cattle and to package and sell garden seeds. Among their many inventions were the buzz saw, washing machine, metal pen point, clothespin and flat broom. It is said that, in proportion to its size, no other group has invented as much.

Order, cleanliness and simplicity also characterized Shaker life. Stressing spiritual concerns, the Believers dressed simply, ate plain food and furnished their rooms sparsely. They built furniture and tools with clean, functional lines. But they also enjoyed singing and formalized dancing in their frequent worship meetings. Many of their hymns express a joyful spirit, as in this verse:

We love to dance, we love to sing
We love to taste the living spring,
We love to feel our union flow,
While round, and round, and round we go.

Begun in 1826, the Shaker settlement at Sodus was the nineteenth and last established in America; with its 150 members it was also the smallest in New York State. When the Sodus Canal Company planned to build a canal through their property, the Shakers felt that would bring the outside world too close to them. In 1837 they moved to Sonyea where they bought 1,670 acres of prime farmland from Dr. Daniel H. Fitzhugh. Ironically, it was but four years later that the Genesee Valley Canal came within yards of this property, but from a practical standpoint their choice was fortunate. The land was fertile, Keshequa Creek supplied water power, and the canal provided transportation for their produce. They later bought additional land in West Sparta and Mt. Morris. They soon prospered by raising wheat, oats, corn and vegetables as well as cattle, sheep and horses. Straw suitable for their unique flat brooms grew on the creek's flatlands, and fruits and berries graced their hills.

The community consisted of two groups called "families" who occupied buildings in what were termed the East House and West House. Besides meeting houses, dormitories and office buildings, these included sewing houses, laundries, barns, tool houses and carriage houses, plus a schoolhouse, dairy, icehouse, sawmill, gristmill and others—a total of thirty buildings.

The Sonyea group's financial success was not without some setbacks. They underwent floods and several fires, one destroying seven buildings. One of the two "families" incurred debts due to an unwise purchase of land, and some trustees once absconded with communal funds. Nevertheless, a member of a visiting delegation could write, "... with all the inconveniences they have had to endure, they seemed to move along as happily as those in older Societies who are blest with more liberal advantages. At any rate, they are lovely people ..."

Through the years, their Valley neighbors came to respect these folk for their industry, frugality and orderliness. Though they did not care to be "in the world," the Shakers were generous to others in time of need. Outsiders at first attended Shaker services as a form of entertainment, though a Mt. Morris citizen has recorded, "it (the dancing) was very interesting and quite solemn. I never heard a disturbance while I was there." When the Believers realized that people came merely as curiosity-seekers, they no longer allowed spectators.

Shaker societies cared for foster children, both with the idea of doing good and with the hope of gaining converts. Although the Sonyea group brought up fifty children in its fifty-eight years, not one stayed on as an adult. Chiefly because of dwindling membership, this colony was forced to close and joined the settlement at Watervliet, New York, in 1895. William P. Letchworth, as a prominent worker for the State Board of Charities, had long been interested in the Sonyea society's care of orphans; it was largely through his efforts that the State bought their land as the site for Craig Colony for Epileptics.

In 1897 workers digging under what had been a Shaker Dormitory struck a large marble slab with inscriptions carved on it. A man who had formerly belonged to the society identified it as the group's Sacred Fountain Stone, also called the Lord's Stone and the Prayer Stone. The writing on one side recorded the marker's having been erected in Groveland in 1843 by divine command. The other side bore a message from the Deity saying that it marked a holy spot.

The Shakers had placed the stone on a plot called the Sacred Ground, or the Fountain. Twice a year the community met around it for special ceremonies. This custom was later discontinued, the stone hidden and eventually buried. After being unearthed, it was kept at Craig Colony some years, then displayed in the Shaker Museum in Old Chatham, New York, until 1976 when it was added to an exhibit concerning the Sonyea Shakers in the Livingston Historical Society Museum in Geneseo. There are very few Shakers still living. But several of their buildings still stand at Sonyea, testaments to good workmanship.

150

SOURCES

Andrews, Edward D., "The New York Shakers and Their Industries"

Blinn, H. C., "Diary of the Ministry's Journey to New Lebanon and Groveland"

Kamer, Fran, "The Shakers at Sonyea"

Livingston Republican, Oct. 27, 1892

Melcher, Marguerite, *The Shaker Adventure*

Patchett, Ann, *Historically Speaking*

Parsons, Levi and Rockfellow, eds., *Centennial Celebration, Mt. Morris*

Scherer, John L., "The Dissolution of a Shaker Community"

Smith, James H., *History of Livingston County, N. Y.*

Shaker Worship, the Dance

Frances Willard's "No Small Jangle"

When Frances E. Willard (1839–1898) was preceptress, or principal, of Genesee Wesleyan Seminary in Lima, she was asked to speak at Commencement exercises. She replied that she would have done so gladly if she had been a man, but women were not allowed this privilege, and she "would not face the grim visage of public prejudice." Yet later as president of the National Woman's Christian Temperance Union, she delivered an average of one speech a day for ten years, lecturing in every United States town of ten thousand or more citizens.

Born in Churchville, New York, Frances grew up in Ohio and Wisconsin. She graduated from Northwestern Female College in Evanston, Illinois, and taught natural science there. After a teaching stint at Pittsburgh Female College, she began her two years at Genesee Wesleyan Seminary in 1866.

In her autobiography, *Glimpses of Fifty Years*, Miss Willard quoted from a journal which reveals much of the person she was when she arrived at Lima. As a Westerner, she was somewhat in awe of the Seminary's history of prominent graduates; but, a Methodist, she was thrilled to be part of the oldest seminary of the Methodist Church. (Its associated institute, Genesee College, later became the nucleus of Syracuse University.) Arriving with her father on the stage from Avon, she was delighted with the "pastoral peace of the historic village nestling among the hills of Genesee." Although the school was co-educational, her work was with the young ladies included, besides the duties of preceptress, teaching rhetoric and composition. Her first duty was to welcome newcomers, of whom two were Indians from a Seneca reservation. "Have had several homesick girls to look after. I pray I may do them good," she wrote in her first week. A later entry reads, "Girls, girls, girls! Dear me, it is no small undertaking to be elder sister to

151

the whole 180 of them, but . . . I like them all." She took "sweet counsel" with a colleague whose spirit was "tremulous with aspirations toward God." And she reported with evident approval that a housekeeper in the dormitory kissed her cheek, saying, "You dear little kitten, you. If anybody hurts you, I'll bite 'em, that's all!"

Yet between the lines of this record of Victorian decorum lie a few hints of the woman Frances Willard would become. Her pride in women's abilities comes through the entry: "Girls are ten times as quick as boys. . . . I should think the boys would take hold and study for shame." Her forceful nature is fore-shadowed in her refusal to lock the door of her dormitory at ten every night and unlock it at five-thirty every morning. When told that the preceptresses had always done this, she rejoined, "More's the pity. It is the janitor's business." This made "no small jangle" among the faculty, she reported. Despite her outward conformity to women's prescribed role, she noted, "I should have made a traveler if I had been a man—as I sometimes wish I had been."

After a trip to Europe during which she studied at the Collège de France and the Sorbonne, Willard was elected president of Evanston College for Women (successor to Northwestern Female College), becoming the first woman president of any United States college. When Northwestern University absorbed her college, she was the University's first dean of women as well as professor of esthetics. Much as she enjoyed this work, her disapproval of the University's lack of supervision of women students caused her to resign in 1873.

A woman's temperance crusade in Chicago which occurred at this same time so impressed her that she felt impelled to work for the cause. Since her father had signed a temperance pledge in Churchville years before, liquor had never been served in her home; also her devotion to Methodist principles made her a temperance advocate. Frightened though she was to speak before a crowd, she addressed rallies in Chicago churches. Never having been in a saloon, she entered many to take part in revival-type meetings at which "wicked men wept and prayed." She turned down offers of teaching positions to follow what she termed "the divine call to my life work." Within the year she was made president of the Chicago Woman's Christian Crusade on Temperance. She became successively secretary of the Illinois and national organizations and then president of the national body in 1881.

In this work she developed into an effective speaker and a forceful administrator. During her tenure the Woman's Christian Temperance Union grew to 250,000 members in 10,000 units. In 1883 Miss Willard founded the World's WCTU, which before her death in 1898, numbered 300,000 members in thirty-five countries.

Excessive drinking was widespread in nineteenth-century America. Hard liquor was usually served with meals as an aid to digestion; it was customarily served in all levels of society on festive occasions and public events. In 1829 the Secretary of War estimated that three-fourths of the country's laborers drank at least four ounces of distilled spirits a day. In his *History of the Town of Conesus*, William Boyd observed:

> In the early days of the town it was not singular to see all the ministers use liquor before going to Church, as they thought in those days it helped the service by enlightening the intellect and gave them smartness in speaking. Whenever there was an ordination or any important ceremony to take place, the "little brown jug" was also found there to assist them. It was not an unusual thing to see a minister under the influence of same.

Temperance societies were formed early in the century and after 1825 were allied with the forces of evangelical Christianity, gradually shifting from the goal of temperance to abstinence and prohibition of the liquor trade. Membership in temperance societies was originally limited to men; women belonged to auxiliaries. Frances Willard's WCTU was the first national organization to include women on a national scale.

With its slogans of "Home Protection" and "For God and Home and Native Land," this crusade merged its cause with the images of home and family so sacred to Victorians. The white ribbon bow that its members wore was a symbol not only of abstinence but of middle-class virtue. The high moral tone of this campaign made it respectable for women to act in public. Willard foresightedly included woman suffrage in the organization's aims primarily because the divorce and property laws then made women who were dependent on alcoholic men helpless victims of "Demon

Rum." Dedicated to women's participation in all aspects of life, she widened the WCTU's scope to include agitation in favor of better schools, prison reform, peace, nutrition education and kindergartens and against child labor, juvenile delinquency, prostitution and gambling.

When Congress voted to place Frances Willard's statue in the Capitol rotunda, she was described as "the first woman of the nineteenth century, the most beloved character of her time." If it seems unfortunate that she did not live to see passage of the Eighteenth Amendment in 1920, it is just as well she was not alive to experience repeal of the "noble experiment" in 1933. But, idealist that she was, if she were alive today, she would probably believe that her cause would rise again.

SOURCES

Boyd, William, *History of the Town of Conesus, Livingston County, N. Y.*
Rorabaugh, W. J., *The Alcoholic Republic: An American Tradition*
Willard, Frances E., *Glimpses of Fifty Years, the Autobiography of an American Woman*
"Willard, Frances," McGraw Hill Encyclopedia of World Biography

Some People and Circumstances
Out of the Ordinary

The Pampered Pet

When Peter McNab was a boy in Caledonia, an uncle determined that he should become a minister, causing his mother to favor him over her seven other children. Peter wanted to marry a young woman who was not up to his family's standards for a clergyman's wife, but she turned the tables by jilting him. At about this time in the 1840's, McNab preached his first sermon and decided he was not suited for the ministry. For either or both of these reasons, he went to bed and stayed there the next twenty years.

In all that time his mother waited on him "hand and foot," even though her husband had died young, leaving her with the eight children to support. Musically gifted, Peter practiced the flute daily. In fact, it was his love of music that got him out of bed. When the family acquired an organ, he could not resist the temptation to steal downstairs to see it. Hearing his footsteps, the others at first thought the sound was made by their pet lamb, which had the freedom of the house, and were astonished to see Peter vertical. From that day on, he lived normally.

When he and his former fiancee were about eighty years old, relatives put the pair in touch, and they began to write to each other. Living in California, she sent him a gold ring. After Peter had outlived his mother and uncle, a nephew supported him; a woman relative willed him money; and when he became blind a neighbor woman read the Bible to him. Perhaps his always having been pampered contributed to his long life, for in 1920 he died at age 100.

"Which of You Children Did It?"

"I suppose no one stood higher than he in Mt. Morris," G. Wells Root recalled. He referred to R. F. Hawes, teacher of the Mt. Morris district school. "He was a member of the Presbyterian Church and a fine gentleman," Root continued. Hawes had boarded with his parents, sharing a room with his pupil and was "such a perfect enthusiast and so full of mathematics" that Mr. Root claimed that he could not have helped getting a good education. The schoolmaster also played trombone in a brass band "so that you would think it was a death struggle going on."

Two incidents of his school days stood out in Mr. Root's memory. One morning the bell from the tower of a private (and rival) school in the village appeared in the district school's outhouse. Much annoyed at such mischief, Mr. Hawes questioned his students, making each one raise his hand to affirm that he did not know who had done it, and all did so.

Another time someone surreptitiously fired an old cannon in the village, breaking windows in houses nearby. The village authorities offered a reward for information about the culprit but to no avail.

Years later Mr. Hawes visited Root and his wife. Re-living old times, Hawes described how he and a friend had re-located the schoolbell. What is more, they had also fired the cannon, using a fuse which delayed the explosion until, as sober and proper adults, they were safely eating oysters in Mosley's saloon.

The Elder Who Prayed for Snakebites

There was once a family in Conesus who were looked down upon by the proper people of the town as what the historian, William Boyd, called "a perfect nuisance to civilized society." When a son in this family was bitten by a rattlesnake and, fearing death began to repent his misspent life, Elder Wright was called to come and pray with him. The elder after conversing with the victim became satisfied that the young man was "pretty sure of heaven if he did not live too long."

Then in a long address to the Almighty, Elder Wright outlined the boy's past sins and moved on to list those of the other members of the family. He concluded his petition with this appeal:

> O Lord, do send more snakes in the neighborhood. Jo had been bit, and it had brought him to a sense of his sins and to repentance. Lord, send more rattlesnakes! O Lord, let them bite the old man and the old woman. Thou knowest who and what they are. O Lord, send snakes and let them bite Jonathan; let them bite Jim; let them bite all the family. Then and not until then will they repent and turn to Thee. Amen.

Table-Top Surgery

An operation which it was said had never before been attempted was performed in Geneseo in 1844. The patient was Bushrod W. Woodruff, a local newspaper publisher. For some years he had had a tumor on his neck which gradually closed in on his windpipe and was beginning to hinder his breathing. Woodruff and all who knew him realized that it would eventually kill him, but everyone thought nothing could be done about it.

Everyone, that is, except James S. Wadsworth. He came to Woodruff's house and suggested that he have surgery, appealing to him to undertake it if for no other reason than "in the interest of science." Woodruff naturally enough hesitated, since anesthesia was not yet generally used and whiskey was often ineffective as a pain-killer. But Wadsworth said, "If you will submit to an operation, I will bring a talented young surgeon from Albany at my own expense. I am sure he can remove the tumor and save your life." Woodruff agreed.

One summer day a Dr. Webster arrived, laid the patient on the dining room table and, with the help of several local physicians, began the surgery. He worked for a few minutes at cutting away the tumor until Woodruff fainted. When the patient was given a strengthening drink and revived, Webster resumed work as long as he could until Woodruff fainted again. This continued for six hours. During all this time, according to Mrs. Woodruff, her husband never once spoke or even groaned. Dr. Webster later sent the tumor to a Paris medical museum. Well might he have been proud of his feat, for B. W. Woodruff lived fifty years more to the age of eighty-seven.

The Judge Does a Kindness

On the day of his wedding Chester Harding was arrested for debt and thrown into the Caledonia jail. Hardship was nothing new to this young man whose father had kept his family poor by incessantly working to build a perpetual motion machine. After serving as a drummer in the War of 1812, Chester had gone to Caledonia where he barely made a living by making chairs. He operated a tavern after being released from prison and, as he said, "paid off old debts by making new ones."

The sheriff was about to imprison Harding as a debtor a second time when Willard H. Smith, Livingston County's first judge, hid him in a cellar and secretly supplied him with food from a Friday until a Sunday morning. Then, knowing that no arrest on a civil process could be made on the Sabbath, the judge let his captive out of hiding, telling him to "run for it."

Thirty years later when the two men met again for the first time, they were passengers on a Lake Erie steamboat, and Chester Harding was a world-famous portrait painter. After so unceremoniously leaving Caledonia, he had worked his way on a raft down the Allegheny to Pittsburgh. Work there as a housepainter gave him money enough to take his wife and baby away from Caledonia by stealth. Penniless again, he operated a sign-painting business until the day when an itinerant painter made portraits of him and his wife and set him on this career. Seeing them, Harding used sign paints for a likeness of his wife which was so good that he was "frantic with delight."

Study at the Philadelphia Academy was followed by wide demand for his work. It was so popular with Bostonians in 1822 that the great Gilbert Stuart jealously referred to his rival's renown as "the Harding fever." While visiting in England Harding received commissions from members of the nobility, and in the United States he painted Presidents Madison, Monroe and Adams as well as Gen. William T. Sherman, Daniel Webster, Henry Clay and John Marshall.

Yet the conversation between Harding and Judge Smith that day on Lake Erie centered on memories of Caledonia. Harding declared that his first year of marriage in the house he had built in Caledonia was the most satisfactory time of his life.

A Stubborn Man

Shortly before what was to have been Charles Wheeler's wedding, a friend prankishly hid his coat and hat, whereupon Charles vowed never to wear either piece of clothing or to marry.

It would seem that the trickster did his intended bride a favor, for Wheeler became "the Groveland hermit." Living in a hovel, he operated a farm he had inherited and never left Groveland. He raised what was claimed as the largest pair of steers known to the world and sold them to the nation's Centennial Exposition in Philadelphia for $2,500. Disregarding advice to bank the money at interest, he put more than $2,000 in a checking account where it remained $2,000 for more than thirty years.

What a Gal Was Dancing Sal

Sauntering past an East Henrietta church one morning, Dancing Sal took a liking to a stylish horse hitched to a fine buggy. Since its owner was in church, she drove it away unseen. When she stopped for dinner in a wayside tavern the next day, the proprietor reported her theft to the town constable. He gave chase but did not catch up with her until the next Tuesday in Caneadea Center,

Allegany County. There she was taken to a tavern and shut in a bedroom with a guard at the door. As a double precaution against her possible escape, her clothes were taken away.

That night Sal made a rope of her blanket and lowered herself out the window. Wrapped only in the blanket, she hitched a horse to the stolen buggy and resumed her travel. But she soon found that in the dark she had appropriated a much slower horse than her first choice. To get it back, she stopped at a farmhouse and roused the farmer, telling him that she needed to find a doctor to treat a sudden illness and that a drunken hostler had hitched the wrong horse for her. Believing this a matter of life or death, the farmer went with her to the tavern and harnessed the stolen horse all without disturbing the constable's slumber. Next morning Sal went into a home which was temporarily empty and dressed in clothes she found.

The constable traced her to the outskirts of Pittsburgh and there lost the trail. But she eventually returned to Rochester where she was arrested with sixty dollars in gold in her possession. They say that she fought like a tiger to resist arrest.

The Calaboguers

Very little has been recorded about the Calaboguers of Conesus, and, as memories of them fade into oblivion, an aura of mystery begins to surround these people.

First, there is the question of how they were named. They lived in the valley which runs from Conesus Center to Webster's Crossing called Calabogue or Calabogue Hollow. The most likely explanation of the place name is that it derives from a man's name, Calvin Bogue. Early in the town's history, he came to cut shingles on shares from timber growing on Marrowback Hill. He brought in workers, some from the Hudson Valley and some illegally from Canada, who would ask where they could find Calvin Bogue, or Cal Bogue. Eventually the name, Calabogue, became attached to the place and its people.

In his history of Conesus, William Boyd reported that settlers on the Marrowback Hill suffered severely from the famine of 1816, some becoming insane. Carl Carmer described Calaboguers in

Listen for a Lonesome Drum as a "wild lot, inbred, uneducated, their tempers undisciplined by any kind of law . . . the hillbillies of upstate." He characterized a woman of the group as sullen, fierce and uncivilized, adding, "but she moved with the grace of a bobcat."

Townspeople who remember the Calaboguers are less derogatory and dramatic in their descriptions. According to several, most of them were hard-working and honest. Poor they unquestionably were—one account has them living in shacks by the railroad tracks which were so cold in winter that to keep warm the children slept on piles of horse manure. They are said to have been superstitious, and a Calaboguer is recalled as saying, "I'm strong, but my blood is strange in my arm."

SOURCES

The Pampered Pet
Harmon, Isabel F., "The Early Families of Caledonia"

Which of You Children Did It?
Parsons, Levi and Rockfellow, Samuel, eds., *Mt. Morris Centenary*

The Elder Who Prayed for Snakebites
Boyd, William P., *The History of Conesus*

Table-Top Surgery
Livingston County Historical Society, *Annual Report, 1918*

The Judge Does A Kindness
"Harding, Chester," *Dictionary of American Biography*
Livingston County Historical Society, *Annual Report, 1883*

A Stubborn Man
Denison, Frances H., Scrapbook

What A Gal Was Dancing Sal
Letchworth, William P., Papers

The Calaboguers
Carmer, Carl, *Listen for a Lonesome Drum*
Conesus residents, Telephone interviews
Livingston County Historical Society, *Annual Report, 1883*

Friends of Progress at Sodus Bay

Theories of the French philosopher, Charles Fourier, inspired the formation of five socialistic communities in Genesee Country in the 1840's. They were established at Sodus Bay, Clarkson, North Bloomfield, Honeyoye Falls and Wiscoy. Fourier aimed at nothing less than abolishing evil by changing the nature of work to make it gratifying. He envisioned a society in which work would be uncompelled and made attractive by being done cooperatively.

Identifying in human nature twelve basic passions leading to 810 character traits, Fourier proposed that people form communities of twice that number, or 1,620 members. This grouping, he reasoned, would include every possible trait and this diversity lead to happiness. He further planned that these communities be divided into groups and subgroups according to types of labor with each person working at various occupations and changing jobs frequently. Both labor and profit would be divided fairly among all. By so arranging people's activities, he believed that all their "passions" would be satisfied and harmony would prevail.

The decade of the forties was a time of spiritual unrest in the United States. Fourier's vision of Utopia swept through the northeastern states like a religious revival. Albert Brisbane with Horace Greeley's help promoted the cause in America, attracting such leaders as James Russell Lowell, John Greenleaf Whittier and Margaret Fuller. Fourierism was similar to Robert Owen's socialist experiment in Indiana and inspired the Transcendentalist community of Brook Farm in Masachusetts which Ralph Waldo Emerson and Bronson Alcott endorsed. Two members of Brook Farm traveled across New York State lecturing on Fourierism, and one of them wrote of the people of Western New York, "There is more wealth, refinement, freedom of thought, general intelligence here than among either our village or farming population in New

England. They are not so much cursed by a straight-jacket Puritanic piety."

But Fourier's ideas, which the historian, Mark Halloway, has termed "sublime madness and the occasional gleam of sanity," may have had too much of French subtlety and complexity for practical Yankees. American Fourierists applied his concepts piecemeal. They wasted their work and money on poorly-planned ventures, disregarding Fourier's insistence on forming groups of at least 1,620 people and amassing adequate capital. Only three of the more than forty communities lasted more than two years.

The Sodus Bay commune was typical in that it lasted two years to the month, from 1844 to 1846. It was situated on the two-square- mile tract previously owned by the Shaker group which had moved to Sonyea in Groveland. The Friends of Progress, as the Fourierists called themselves, numbered about 100 families from the Rochester area. While most men were farmers and laborers, there were also ministers, doctors and teachers represented and, as it happened, a large number of shoemakers. Each member paid fifty dollars or the equivalent in goods per share of stock, many having sold all they owned to enter into this "heaven on earth."

At first the group's prospects looked bright, for the bay teemed with fish and their land included good fields, orchards and woodland as well as a gristmill and sawmill. The men added a lodging house, blacksmith shop and pier. Although some families lived alone and some in groups, cooking, washing and caring for the sick were done cooperatively. Life in the first few months, however, was chaotic because too many people joined the colony before adequate housing or industries were set up. Also in meetings held to design a constitution, so much time was spent in discussing political philosophy that other aspects of community life were ignored. According to the historian, Arthur Bestor, Jr., the Sodus group simplified Fourier's scheme of apportioning work and distributing income to such an extent that his beliefs are not to blame for the community's failure.

Many other things went wrong. A drought made both mills useless. Because of lack of funds, there were not enough cattle, and milk had to be rationed. Two families were often crowded into one room. Typhoid fever struck. Farming took so much time and effort that none was left for other industries. All these trials naturally led to so many disagreements and resentments that it is perhaps a wonder that the experiments lasted as long as two years.

As so often happens, seemingly minor matters brought about the end—a sorry series of dismissals and withdrawals. Disagreement over whether or not children should be taught strict observance of the Sabbath led to a battle of personalities between conservatives and liberals. As Bestor has noted, "A multitude of little events, apparently irrelevant, were doubtless charged with the passions engendered by a greater conflict." What is the significance of the experiment of the Friends of Progress? It may be that Utopia is hard to find.

SOURCES

Bestor, Jr., Arthur E., *American Phalanxes*
_____, *Backwoods Utopias: The Sectarian and Owenite Phases of Communitarian Socialism in America 1663–1829*
Cross, Whitney R., *The Burned-over District*
Halloway, Mark, *Heavens on Earth*

Rev. Algernon Crapsey,
Prophet and Protestant

The arrival in Rochester of Rev. Algernon Crapsey (1847–1927) was an obscure event. He came to the city in 1879 to be rector of St. Andrew's Church, a small impoverished Episcopal Church parish on Averill Avenue. This priest could, of course, not know that twenty-seven years later people around the world would think of Rochester of as the city where he was deposed for heresy.

It was as a pastor that Dr. Crapsey first revitalized St. Andrew's Church. Ministering to the everyday needs of the working people in the neighborhood, he became the servant of the poor, the ill and dying and those in prison or any other trouble. He founded St. Andrew's Brotherhood, an ecumenical mutual benefit society for men, which grew into a national organization. With his wife, the former Adelaide Trowbridge, he founded Rochester's first kindergarten and kindergarten teacher training school as well as a night school of domestic science and mechanical arts. Besides raising nine children, Mrs. Crapsey led a woman's group in sewing clothes for the needy, served as organist of St. Andrew's and was her husband's partner in all his service to others. This work attracted people of all levels of income and social status to St. Andrew's until it became the fourth largest parish in the Diocese of Western New York.

A scholar and eloquent preacher, Dr. Crapsey not only could make profound truths understandable but also related theology to the practice of the Christian faith. His conducting a mission at St. Philip's Church in New York City, one attended only by Negroes, was an advance in interracial relations of that time. He later conducted missions, led retreats and preached throughout the country and in Canada. His concern for social justice caused

Crapsey to be chosen president of Rochester's Citizens Political Reform Association.

In 1895 Rev. Mr. Crapsey preached in the Third Presbyterian Church of Rochester, which, in itself, was then a breach of Episcopal Church discipline. His bishop, Rt. Rev. William D. Walker, had forbidden him to do so, but Crapsey responded that, since the members of Third Church were within the geographical boundaries of his parish, he had the right to preach to them. By this time, Crapsey's earlier idealism had given way to considerable disillusion. Experience, including European travel, had convinced him that the Christian Church was decadent and dying, its voice irrelevant to the modern world. In his sermon to the Presbyterians, he contended that the Church had falsified Jesus' teaching by changing it from a way of life to a formal and arbitrary doctrine.

While lecturing on theology to a group of Canadian clergymen, Crapsey was attacked as unorthodox. He replied that in his belief, "All the theology of worth to man was theology brought down to human need. Whether Jesus was the Eternal Son of God or not was of no consequence. It was the human Jesus with his human insight into human life that mattered." Later in an address on Christian unity, this minister angered many of his hearers by claiming that the disunion of contemporary Christianity would have disappointed Jesus. Published as a tract, this essay was reviewed in national publications, with the result that its author was severely criticized by the "High Church" faction among Episcopalians and lauded by their "Broad church" element as well as by liberal members of other denominations.

Nevertheless, the parishioners of St. Andrew's marked the twenty-fifth anniversary of the Crapseys' coming to Rochester with a week-long celebration in 1904. Their rector was all but canonized in a sermon; he was given a letter of commendation and a coin-filled loving cup; and praise was heaped on him by the city's clergy and press. It was a happy commemoration of this priest's years of dedicated service—and a calm before the storm.

The next year Rev. Mr. Crapsey delivered a series of talks at Sunday evening services on the relation of the Church to the state. In the last of these, he contended that neither the virgin birth or resurrection of Jesus were literally true, but were myths told as means of describing His greatness. Thus, he claimed, the Christian creeds are not to be considered historical statements. He believed that Jesus was divine (God-like), but opposed His being deified (identified with God). Crapsey once wrote that his application of scholarly criticism to New Testament reports—the first public instance in this country—meant that to him "Jesus was the Son of God in a far higher sense than He had ever been before; He was the Son of God, not by divine miracle, but by divine law; He was the Son of the Father because He was the life of the Father manifested in the world."

Widely reported in newspapers around the world, this interpretation of the historic creeds caused Bishop Walker the next day to demand a retraction, which Dr. Crapsey refused to give. A Committee appointed to investigate the matter produced a majority report that there was not enough evidence the warrant the Church's taking action against him.

Despite this outcome, Bishop Walker in April, 1906, placed the priest on trial for heresy before the court of the Diocese of Western New York for having declared and taught doctrines contrary to those of the Church. Accompanied by his daughter, Adelaide, and his lawyer, Rev. Mr. Crapsey reported to a court convened in St. James Church, Batavia. So many visitors attended this historic event that sessions were soon moved to the Genesee County courthouse. Witnesses for the prosecution included noted clergymen, one of whom held that the defendant's Christ-like character made his crime all the greater. Testifying against Dr. Crapsey was a priest who had applied for his rectorship if he should be deposed or resign it. Equally distinguished Church leaders spoke in their colleague's defense, but in May the jury declared him guilty of heresy and violation of ordination vows.

Denied an appeal, Dr. Crapsey was suspended from the performance of spiritual duties in his parish. Although he could have remained on the staff performing social service only, he wrote the bishop a letter of renunciation of his ministry. In what the *Rochester Evening Post* called "a spiritual classic," he wrote in part:

It is to me more than meat and drink to have the right to be with my people in every critical hour of their lives, to give them in the name of the living God courage to live and courage to die. . . . To leave this daily ministry to such a people is to break my heart.

But better a broken heart than a life made false and loathsome by
cowardly retraction.

Without mentioning his deposition, Rev. Mr. Crapsey preached to his people for the last time in December, 1906. He and his
family were forced to leave their home of twenty-seven years
where six of their children had been born and two had died.
William Rossiter Seward, who was not then a member of St.
Andrew's, underwrote the cost of a home for them, and loyal
friends gave their labor to build it nearby on Averill Avenue. From
it Dr. Crapsey went to preach in the city's theaters, and the St.
Andrew Brotherhood continued to help people in need. Mrs.
Crapsey made smocked dresses for little girls, first for the family's
support, later giving jobs to a group of neighborhood women,
which she named the Guild of the Lily.

Dr. Crapsey was a delegate to the International Peace Conference at the Hague in 1907 and for several years worked as a State
parole officer, at one time in the reformatory, Industry, outside
Rochester. These years were saddened by the deaths of his son,
Philip, and his daughter, Adelaide. She had written poems in a
form she invented called the cinquain, consisting of five unequal
lines. When Claude Bragdon, a family friend, published them after
her death, they earned a lasting place in early twentieth-century
American poetry. Before the Rochester Historidal Society and the
Rochester Academy of Sciences, Dr. Crapsey delivered an address
in tribute to the anthropologist, Lewis Henry Morgan. Of the six
books he wrote in his later years, the final one was an autobiography titled (hopefully and to-date accurately) *The Last of the
Heretics.*

Algernon Crapsey never renounced his basic loyalty to the
Church. In his letter of renunciation he had written to clergy who
shared his views, "Let no one be dismayed. Let every man stand in
his place—speak his mind boldly, and the truth will soon have such
a multitude of witnesses that all in the Church may hear. . . . I
exhort my brethren of like belief to stay where they are." He
believed that the decision against him, while final for him, was not
final for the Church. And he had the bitter-sweet experience of
seeing the time come when individual interpretation of the
Church's creeds would be commonplace.

SOURCES

Crapsey, Algernon, *The Last of the Heretics*

"Crapsey, Algernon", *Dictionary of American Biography*

Swanton, Carolyn, "Dr. Algernon S. Crapsey: Religious Reformer"

Some Spiritualist Seekers

The historian, Whitney Cross, has stated that many Western New Yorkers of the early nineteenth century were "given to unusual beliefs, peculiarly devoted to crusades aimed at the perfection of mankind . . . " One of the most popular of these crusades was Spiritualism—the belief that spirits of the dead can communicate with the living through persons called mediums.

The Spiritualism Movement began in the Valley with the "Rochester rappings" in 1848. They were the development of a trick which the teen-age sisters, Margaretta and Kate Fox, played on their mother in which they claimed that rapping noises were messages sent them by a murder victim. Their older sister, Mrs. Leah Fish, took them from their home in Hydesville, New York, to live with her in Rochester where they gave seances by calling out letters of the alphabet to which the spirit ostensibly rapped once for "Yes" and twice for "No." Four hundred people flocked to Rochester's Corinthian Hall to see the young ladies' first public performance, and a new religion was underway.

Among the first persons caught up in this enthusiasm were Isaac and Amy Post, prominent members of the city's Abolitionist forces and friends of Susan B. Anthony and Frederick Douglass. Mr. Post published a book which he believed had been dictated to him by Washington, Jefferson, Franklin and other leaders. (It is not recorded if anyone had the affrontery to point out to this widely respected gentleman that the opinions of all the great men markedly resembled his own.) Despite the Fox sisters' sensationalism, the sect attracted many sober and thoughtful people to annual meetings held in Rochester up through the late 1870's. After the Fox sisters made a country-wide tour, the movement grew until Spiritualists claimed more than a million adherents to the faith. In darkened rooms throughout the land tables were mysteriously tipped and cryptic messages tapped out. Horace Greeley, the reformer-editor, was converted, and the writers, James Fenimore Cooper and William Cullen Bryant, as well as the singer, Jenny Lind, were among those who attended seances. It was not until 1888 that Margaretta admitted that she and Kate had made the rappings by cracking their toe joints.

Spiritualism gave rise in 1873 to a macabre incident involving an Avon mother and daughter who were mediums. The daugher had predicted that after her "going out," or death, she would be restored to life, and, when she did die, her mother refused to have the body buried. The local sensation this created brought about inspection of the corpse by two county coroners, who asserted that the woman was "dead beyond resurrection until the day when the trump shall sound." In deference to the wishes of the mother and other Spiritualists, the coroners delayed burial for several weeks, which allowed time for newspaper stories with such headlines as "A Horrid Spectacle." Meanwhile, the Spiritualists, claiming that the deceased was merely sleeping, charged thrill-seekers fifty cents apiece to see her.

Within several weeks of this brouhaha, James Brodie, Geneseo correspondent for the *Rochester Daily Chronicle* and *Evening Express*, reported an upsurge of belief in Spiritualism in that town. He reprinted an article from another newspaper which stated:

> Some of the converts are men of good judgment, and their conversion to the new faith excites considerable surprise.
>
> Several months ago one of our well-known and influential citizens and a member of one of our Christian churches ... became carried away with the new doctrine. The gentleman alluded to is a member of an important board in this village, and at one of its meetings a circle was formed around a table when the usual laying-on of hands took place, but without result. ... The disappointment of the evening was accounted for by the "dirty hands" of one the circle.

To this Mr. Brodie added his own attempt "to separate fact from fancy":

> The circle is formed, and after sitting in silence for a few minutes a prominent member of the bar who has represented

Livingston County in the State Legislature and of late developed as a medium, puts his lips down at the table and holds a whispered conversation with the spirits. He soon rises and orders "Jug," the name of one of the spirits, to enter a gentleman who is an officer of our courts and who has also developed into a medium. The "Jug" spoken to is . . . an Indian who lived south of Geneseo some 300 years ago. . . . "Jug" twitches, shuffles his feet under the table as if dancing the green corn dance, beats a tattoo upon the table and tries a war-whoop . . . The usual manner of obtaining answers to questions is then entered into, in which some things occur which have the appearance of mystery.

Brodie did not divulge the name of the "prominent member of the bar," but his identity must have been evident to Geneseoans at the time, for induction shows that it could only have been General James Wood. Former state senator, brigadier general and eminent attorney, James Wood was in 1874 the very model of respectability. Ever since taking over John Young's practice when that gentleman became Governor of New York, Wood had been termed one of the State's ablest jury lawyers. He handled a regiment in more than ten battles of the Civil War. A high ranking Mason and a member of St. Michael's Church, he was president of the Local Board of Geneseo Normal School. This was a man of wide experience, not ordinarily credulous.

Among General Woods's papers there have been found ten slips of paper with questions written on one side and answers on the back. Headed "Questions put to Mrs. Woods's spirit," they obviously represent an attempt by the General to communicate with his wife, Ann, who had died in 1871. They read:

Is Spiritualism, as we call it, a blessing to us who are left on this earth? Yes.

Are our spiritual bodies fashioned like our earthly bodies? No.

Is it distressful to you to be questioned as we are now questioning you? No.

Do you recognize any of us who are in this room? Yes.

Are any of your ideas while you were on this earth as to the spirit world now realized? No.

Is Mrs. Young, your sister on earth, with you in the spirit land? No.

Does your spirit change in any respect when you come near this earth? Yes.

Can you pass at will wherever you choose to in the spirit land? No.

Have you as yet been permitted to see God? Yes.

Would you, if you could, leave the spirit land to come back again to this earth to remain? No.

A concern with spiritualism links the lives of two Rochesterians of the twentieth century, Claude Bragdon and Adelaide Crapsey. Claude Bragdon gave his autobiography the appropriate title, *More Lives Than One*, alluding to his experiences as an architect, stage designer, writer and explorer of the occult. Rochester knew Bragdon primarily as an architect when, from 1901 to 1923, he designed many of its public buildings. The New York Central railroad station, later demolished, is considered his chief work of art. Others are the First Universalist Church, the Chamber of Commerce building, Bevier Memorial Building of Rochester Institute of Technology as well as the portico and sunken garden of Eastman House. Bragdon was designer and art director for fifteen plays produced by the actor, Walter Hampden. His set designs were acclaimed for the symbolic use of color, light and mass.

Through writing many books Claude Bragdon tried to introduce appreciation of the mystic life to Westerners. He was founder and president of the Genesee Chapter of the Theosophy Society, part of a world-wide movement which seeks to learn about reality through mystical experience and through finding esoteric meaning in sacred writings.

Bragdon's second wife, Eugenie, practiced Spiritualism, though she was not a member of the sect. She believed that a spirit sent her messages which she transcribed by automatic writing. When in 1915 she received messages from someone named Adelaide, her husband told her they could only have been sent by the daughter of the renowned Rochester minister, Algernon Crapsey. Bragdon had known and admired Adelaide Crapsey, who had died the previous year. The Bragdons delivered to her parents such consoling messages as "Life has been so full here, and I have known things impossible to the flesh" and "I found here a strange new beginning." Miss Crapsey had written poetry, which Bragdon published in a volume called simply *Poems*. He called her "Rochester's one true poet," and critics have praised her work for its delicate, yet penetrating, beauty.

Belief in Spiritualism appears to some an exercise in self-delusion, to others a phenomenon humans do not yet understand. Dr. Joseph B. Rhine, an authority in parapsychology, has said, that it "represents an important front in (man's) long search ... to achieve that full understanding of and control over his destiny that his happiness requires."

SOURCES

Bragdon, Claude F., *More Lives Than One*
Brodie, William, Scrapbook
Costa, Erville, "Claude F. Bragdon, Architect, Stage Designer and Mystic"
Cross, Whitney R., *The Burned-over District*
Doyle, Sir Arthur Conan, *The History of Spiritualism*
McKelvey, Blake, *Rochester the Water-Power City 1812-1854*
———, Rochester, the Flower City, 1855–1890
"Spiritualism," *Encyclopedia Americana*

Miss Ellen North's Jam Kitchen

When the Geneseo Jam Kitchen was operating, people used to stroll by it simply to enjoy the delicious fragrances floating from it—strawberry, raspberry and currant in the summer, apple and grape in the fall. For an enterprise no larger than it was, it had a remarkably wide market, with sales throughout the United States and in many other countries. It was begun and supervised for many years by Miss Ellen North (1851–1939).

A genteel Victorian lady who was a niece of New York Governor John Young, Miss North was, as she would have said, "a bit hard up for cash" in the Depression year of 1893. Beginning in the kitchen of her home on Geneseo's Main Street, she hired a few women to help her make jams and jellies. As the business grew, she added workrooms to her house and later moved production to a building next door, which she named the Geneseo Jam Kitchen. Its steam boiler was so powerful that heat was piped from it to each building southward for some 100 yards.

By 1899 Miss North employed what a *Livingsotn Republican* article referred to as fifty "hands." A number of women who would not otherwise have worked outside the home worked there where the atmosphere was pleasant and neighborly. At that time the business consumed annually eight and a half tons of cherries, eighteen tons of currants and 300 bushels of strawberries. It took the yield of a sixteen-acre tract of currants on the Mt. Morris flats.

No chemicals or coloring agents were used in Miss North's products—only sugar and the best fruit available, cooked within twelve hours of its having been picked. The recipes were a secret known to only two employees. The Jam Kitchen at one time produced fifty-two products including, besides the standard jams and jellies, orange and grapefruit marmalade, stuffed oranges, plum pudding, sauces, mince meat, pickled pears and peaches, flavoring syrup and brandied fruit. During the Prohibition era Miss North obtained the Federal Government's permission to continue selling brandied conserves and was said to be the only producer who could do this.

Every product was packed in custom-made glass jars. Miss North designed a special jar for jelly so that its contents could be taken out unbroken, something impossible with jars having rounded "hips." Her jar was a rectangle, like a cowbell, and one gentle tap with a knife ejected intact a shimmering edible sculpture.

On sales trips to New York City, Miss North stayed at the Waldorf Hotel and required her customers to come to her. The prestigious firms of Charles and Company, S. S. Pierce and Park and Tilford were among her chief customers. Once when lunching with her at the Waldorf, her sales manager ordered corned beef and cabbage, incurring her indignation at his low-brow choice. A stately woman, she wore an ear trumpet on a gold chain. But when people raised their voices for her benefit, she would draw herself up to her imposing height and reply, "You need not shout. I can hear you perfectly well."

During World War I the United States Army ordered Jam Kitchen jams and jellies in tins by the million. Miss North converted her business to quantity production, but evidently maintained her standard of quality, for many soldiers wrote to ask if she were still unmarried.

When the Government's contracts were cancelled after the war, Miss North had the considerable expense of converting back to glass jars as well as other financial problems. She sold the business during the late twenties, taking a well-earned rest. In a day when few women of her social station ventured beyond the realm of children, church and kitchen, she was a successful businesswoman.

SOURCES

Geneseo residents, Personal interviews
Livingston Republican, June, 29, 1899; Sept. 23, 1937

The Joys and Sorrows of George Eastman

The rise to riches of George Eastman (1854–1932) is a true story that surpasses even the Horatio Alger tales. Two years after the family moved to Rochester from Waterville, New York, George's father died. His mother took in boarders, and at age fourteen George helped with their support by working as a real estate agent's errand boy at three dollars a week. Later he became a junior bookkeeper for the Rochester Savings Bank. At one time considering a trip to Santo Domingo where he would want to take pictures, he took lessons in photography and bought some equipment.

At that time photography was a complicated process. To take pictures outdoors George had to carry about a large camera, tripod, heavy glass plates and holder, a light-proof tent, chemicals and container of water. He simplified picture-taking by producing dry plates through a method of applying to glass a gelatin emulsion which supported light-sensitive chemicals. The Eastman Dry Plate Company, which he founded in 1881, was moderately successful, but he realized that its sales were limited to professional photographers. Experimenting tirelessly, Eastman produced a substitute for glass plates—paper coated with gelatine and photographic emulsion and rolled on a holder. He later overcame problems with this by inventing a flexible celluloid film.

Then in 1888 Eastman introduced the Kodak, a name he invented. This small box camera made photography easily available to amateurs. Widely advertised with the slogan, "You press the button and we do the rest," more than 1,000,000 Kodaks were sold in the first two years. Thomas Edison's invention of motion pictures spurred sales of film; color film was inaugurated in 1928; and technical improvements were made continually over the years. Eastman Kodak Company, formed in 1892, pioneered in market research, developing sales worldwide. It soon became not only Rochester's leading manufacturer but the giant of an immense industry which made photography the educational tool and recreation of millions.

From the beginning George Eastman was generous, giving $50 to Mechanics Institute (later Rochester Institute of Technology) when his salary was less than $60 a month. As he became many times over a millionaire, his gifts were stupendous. Among the first were a dormitory for Hillside Children's Home, a nurses' wing for what became Genesee Hospital, a $3,000,000 campus for the Massachusetts Institute of Technology and gifts to Tuskeegee and Hampton Institutes. An employee's having become incapacitated from an ulcerated tooth influenced Eastman to establish free dental clinics for children in Rochester and five European cities. Besides offering health and accident payments and a savings and loan association, Eastman Kodak firm was the first in the country to give its employees dividends and profit-sharing bonuses.

Eastman's gifts to the University of Rochester, begun in 1903, were climaxed by a $50,000,000-contribution for its river campus, including the School of Medicine and Dentistry and Strong Memorial Hospital. Also bequeathed to the University was his elegant East Avenue mansion and its collection of art masterpieces, including paintings by Rembrandt, Van Dyke, Tintoretto and Hals. In addition he gave Rochester the Eastman School of Music and Eastman Theatre as well as Durand-Eastman Park, the Chamber of Commerce Building and the site of the Community War Memorial. In sum Eastman gave away more than $100,000,000 during his life and $21,000,000 through his will.

Such is the "Kodak King's" public image—that of an ambitious, hardworking and successful industrialist and lavish philanthropist. Basically shy and reserved except with close friends, he adopted a formal manner, hiding his private self behind a "Mr. Businessman" facade. Those who knew him have agreed about only a few of his personal characteristics.

First, it is clear that he was devoted to his mother. Much of his drive for wealth was his desire to compensate her for the hardships she endured in their years of poverty. He was happy when he could install her in a comfortable home at Arnold Park and during the last two years of her life in the beauty and luxury of his East Avenue home. Once, admitting surprise at his vast fortune, he exclaimed, "All I had in mind was to make enough money so that my mother would never have to work again." After her death, he always carried her little gold watch.

Though Eastman had never taken a vacation until he was in his forties, he developed a great liking for outdoor life. With a few close friends, he enjoyed quail-shooting on his North Carolina plantation, pack-train trips in the mountains of the western United States, yachting voyages and African game hunts. Camping delighted him because of his talent for outdoor cooking and designing ways of packing and carrying equipment efficiently.

Eastman's mansion had a four-manual organ with more than 100 ranks of pipes. Every day for twenty-seven years, he had an organist play for him as he breakfasted as well as at evening musicales twice a week. While he was not musically sophisticated, music gave him great joy. Howard Hanson, composer and first permanent dirctor of the Eastman School of Music, observed that for this man "music was a spiritual necessity." His organist, Harold Gleason, has written, "Music seemed to give him a very personal, inner satisfaction which transcended anything I have ever encountered in another person."

In the years when he could afford leisure, Eastman entertained frequently. He gave dinners for celebrities visiting Rochester and sometimes invited them to breakfast. About 100 guests were usually present at his Wednesday and Sunday evening musicals performed by the organist and the Kilbourn String Quartet. These affairs were quite formal, during which Eastman maintained his customary polite and reticent manner. Many who knew him only slightly thought him stiff, humorless and colorless. Claude Bragdon, for one, wrote of him as "a man of steel in an age of steel, a stoic, a slave of duty," adding, "In his later years he worked conscientiously at large-scale entertaining ... (but) there was never any joy in him ... "

What Bragdon and many others did not know was the existence of the Lobster Quartet. This was the name four women called themselves because of their Saturday luncheons with Eastman at which they usually had lobster and always much conversation. They were Katharine Whipple (Mrs. George), wife of the dean of the University of Rochester School of Dentistry; Marion Gleason (Mrs. Harold), wife of Eastman's personal organist and organist of the Eastman School of Music; Nan Bayne-Jones (Mrs. Stanhope), wife of a University of Rochester School of Medicine faculty member; and Mary Folsom (Mrs. Marion), wife of Eastman's right-hand man at Kodak.

These women were young, lively and informal; three had small children; three happened to be from the South. With much in common, they made a natural grouping. Somehow, Eastman made himself a fifth member of their circle. Sometimes he would listen silently, sometimes engage with them in an exchange of views as they chatted about raising children, furnishing their homes, following events in Rochester—whatever was on their minds. He shared with them an interest in women's clothes, subscribing to *Vogue* to learn more about current fashion. Occasionally the talk took a serious turn, as when the right to commit suicide was discussed. Lobster was such a favorite with the four that Eastman once said, "I think you come here just to eat lobster!" whereupon the next week they brought their own lunches: cornmeal mush.

These light-hearted luncheons had to end when Eastman became ill with a debilitating disease of deterioration of the spinal column. In March of 1932 he fatally shot himself, leaving a note, "My work is done. Why wait?" Many were to call this an action typical of the pragmatic "man of steel." But at least one person had other thoughts. Katherine Whipple has recalled, "His household staff— with the best—intentions guarded him so carefully that no one could see him, or, if so, for only a few minutes. When you phoned you could only talk to the butler, the housekeeper or the nurse. If they had let people come to see him, he would have been happier. He felt that his friends had deserted him, that he *wasn't wanted*! Had they been a little more liberal, he might not have committed suicide when he did."

SOURCES

Ackerman, Carl, *George Eastman*
Foster, Abram, "Eastman"
"George Eastman, 1854–1954," *Genesee Country Scrapbook*
Hayes, Catherine D., ed., *The University of Rochester Library Bulletin*
Neblette, C.C., "George Eastman"
Rollick, Jeffrey, Genesee Valley Memories, Recorded Oct. 3, 1976

Father Flaherty—Saint or Devil?

To his admirers he was almost a saint, to his enemies a very devil. He did a great deal of good, but he also took wicked delight in upsetting the Establishment. This controversial figure was the Rev. Charles Flaherty (1856–1939).

The twenty-six-year-old priest came to Mt. Morris as pastor of its Roman Catholic parish, St. Patrick's Church, in 1882. No doubt he began his work with the usual high hopes of a young priest entering his first pastorate. Certainly, he could not know what mingled triumphs and troubles the coming years would bring. Today, while only a few remain who knew him well, nearly everyone who grew up in the area has heard tales about him. He is on his way to becoming a folk hero.

Son of a Baldwinsville, N.Y., miller, Charles Flaherty had graduated from a Canadian college and St. Joseph Provincial Seminary in Troy and served in a Rochester parish. He was ruggedly handsome at twenty-six and was generally admired as a forward-looking administrator and a forceful preacher.

Eleven years later in 1893, Bishop Bernard McQuaid suspended him from the exercise of priesthood. The reason: his being convicted of criminal assault and sentenced to prison. He was found guilty of raping a local girl under the age of sixteen.

The trial consisted of the complainant's unsupported testimony and the defense's efforts to prove that she was untruthful. Father Flaherty's lawyer suggested that she should be taken to the Columbian Exposition, then in progress in Chicago, and "put on exhibition as the very acme of brazen girlhood, as the monumental liar not only of the nineteenth century, but of all ages." A crowded courtroom heard that a certain letter incriminated Father Flaherty, that no such letter existed and that the priest had struck two men.

When the all-male jury brought in a verdict of guilty, the

priest asserted his belief that he had been convicted on perjured testimony. "Liberty is dear to me," he said, "but dearer still is my honor. I could have taken my liberty at any time, but I wish it always to be said of me that I have never abused the confidence of my friends and that when I go down I want to go down fighting with my face to the enemy, as an innocent man and a priest of the altar, asserting my innocence and maintaining my rights." He was sentenced to a seven-and-a-half-year prison term but given a stay to enable him to appeal the charge.

Services in St.Patrick's Church the next Sunday were conducted by a Rochester priest, with Father Flaherty present in the sanctuary but not taking part. At a meeting of his friends that afternoon, he reiterated his innocence and was assured that a large proportion of the congregation was still loyal to him. Money was raised for his support and a committee formed to thank Bishop McQuaid for his backing. By the following Sunday, however, the bishop had appointed the Rev. James Day as pastor.

Presumably it was then that both priests arrived at the church at the same time, each prepared to say Mass. A cocked pistol aimed at him by a sheriff persuaded Father Flaherty otherwise. It was probably also around this time that there was a parade in which both the factions for and against the suspended priest marched—in two different directions! And in 1904 a Father Flaherty Association had badges printed with his picture to advertise what they called their first annual picnic.

It is said that the bishop offered to reinstate Father Flaherty if he would move to another community. When friends advised him to do so, he refused, saying, "I haven't done anything to be ashamed of. They may be ashamed—I'm not." As the result of his appeal, he was given another trial and again convicted. Appealing a second time, he succeeded in having the indictment dismissed for lack of sufficient evidence—this in 1901, eight years after the charges were first made.

Such a legal technicality did not clear Flaherty's name with those who thought him guilty. On the other hand, the Rev. Robert McNamara has stated in his authorized history, *The Diocese of Rochester 1868-1968*, "Highly respected priests who knew the story well . . . were strongly persuaded that the first charges laid against Father Flaherty were untrue and that Bishop McQuaid had been at fault for not standing by him."

So began a series of ambiguous events which were to characterize the rest of this man's long life. Added to the sharp contradictions of his character are the reports, both pro and con, of his actions.

Staying on in Mt. Morris, he kept his identity as a priest, continuing to wear a black frock coat, the Roman collar, usually a long black cloak and invariably a broad-brimmed black homberg hat. He began an intensive study on his own of both law and medicine. It may have been at this time the story went around the village that he had never wanted to be a priest. His mother, people said, had been one of the "old-time" Irish and wanted nothing more than a priest in the family and had overridden his reluctance. There was no source for this tale; it was merely "generally known."

Tall, broad-shouldered and square-jawed, Flaherty was also an expert boxer. John L. Sullivan, one-time world's heavyweight champion, came to Upstate New York for training sessions in those years, where the priest was occasionally his sparring partner. He endeared himself to many Mt. Morris sports fans when he fought Sullivan in an exhibition match there and won the professional's praise as the best amateur he had ever fought.

Father Flaherty adopted as his unofficial parish all the poor people of the area and ministered to them as their doctor and lawyer. Carrying a long knobbed cane (called by one observer a cudgel, by another a shillelagh) and often followed by several stray dogs, he was a frequent sight in the village and on country roads as he went to care for a sick person or to advise someone in trouble with the law.

Local physicians and lawyers were, of course, opposed to an unlicensed person's practicing their professions. Was it, then, the work of enemies or justifiable suspicion that in 1901 brought the priest to trial for the murder by poisoning of a Mt. Morris man? At the height of the trial, Father Flaherty stepped in front of the prosecutor, grabbed the bottle holding the alleged poison and gulped down a good amount. It is at least possible that Flaherty had poisoned the victim and later substituted something harmless in the bottle. He could have prescribed medicine which, taken over a long period, killed the patient, but one drink of which did not harm him. Or he could have prescribed a substance in small amounts and the patient taken an overdose. We do know that the judge directed Father Flaherty's acquittal.

Twice this self-taught healer was indicted for illegal practice of medicine. In 1907 the charge was dismissed. The next year he was convicted and fined $250, an outcome which he appealed.

The crux of these cases was whether Father Flaherty received payment for his care of the sick. This was hard to prove, as many of the poor whom he helped expressed their gratitude in gifts such as farm produce. All too often, families could give him only their undying affection. Yet how could this Good Samaritan have existed for forty-six years with no income? A local barber and the proprietor of a lunch counter, among others, never charged him, and a group of workingmen who lived near him helped by pooling their food purchases with his. Yet this hardly explains how he often took groceries to people in need and how, whenever he had a ton of coal delivered, he told the deliveryman to take half of it to a neighborhood family who could not afford it. His sister in Syracuse sent him special delivery letters several times a week; perhaps they contained money.

Over the years Father Flaherty went on befriending some and offending others. Whenever he heard that someone was ill, he would produce from a medical bag a bottle of medicine which—some say—invariably cured the invalid. In the flu epidemic of 1918, he is said to have gone to homes where no one else would go and not to have lost a patient. A Protestant woman from a neighboring town was one who sought him out. It was whispered, too, that one of his standard medicines was whiskey.

While the doctors could not restrain this non-conformist, the lawyers could at least limit his lawyerly activities to the courts of justices of the peace. Many times when an unlettered farmer or recent immigrant produced a defense based on a tricky loophole, people knew who was behind him. Flaherty visited the courts of Rochester and Livingston County towns nearly every week.

Obviously, he enjoyed baiting the courts. One day the Livingston county clerk was perturbed to learn that a judgment of a Mt. Morris resident was missing from the docket. Father Flaherty returned it the next day, having merely taken it home to study it.

A man pleaded guilty and paid a fine for trapping muskrats one day before the season opened. He should not have admitted his guilt, Father Flaherty told him, as the warden rightfully would have had to bring to court the man's trap with the muskrat still in it to prove him guilty. Defending a friend accused of shooting a pheasant, he asked the accuser if he was sure it was a pheasant and was told it was. The priest then produced a feather, asking if it was a pheasant feather and received the same answer. "Wrong!" he replied, "It's the feather of a partridge!"

Many such incidents endeared this modern Robin Hood to the common man and infuriated county officials. "He has for years handled legal cases in courts other than those of record," the *Livingston Republican* reported in 1922, "in spite of efforts to discourage him from doing so." Regrettably, the article did not describe the efforts. But it did give the priest the dubious distinction of having in the previous thirty years been more often on the court records of the county as the defendant in a criminal action that anyone else.

Flaherty made the headlines that year in the aftermath of another court case. One man was charged with shooting at and narrowly missing another in a Mt. Morris restaurant. His trial was long delayed because the principal witness for the offense had mysteriously disappeared. When eventually he was found, the defendant immediately pleaded guilty. The district attorney forthwith charged Father Flaherty with bribery of a witness and compounding a felony. He accused him of inducing the witness to go to Canada and stay there until his testimony would do no harm. He claimed Flaherty had furnished this man with clothing, whiskey (and this during Prohibition) and transportation and promised him board, lodging, care and maintenance, knowing that his testimony was necessary for the case against the gunman. Predictably, Father Flaherty pleaded not guilty, claiming that the county court had transgressed its powers in allowing the taking of testimony about events alleged to have taken place in Canada, over which New York State courts have no jurisdiction. This time the jury could not agree, and the indictment was dropped. For the fifth time Charles Flaherty went free.

But four years later the tide went against him. "In his whole career with the courts of Livingston County," ran a newspaper report in January, 1926, "this was the first time that the keys of the jail were turned on him as a prisoner." He was charged with causing the death of a young woman by performing an illegal operation on her. As one of his supporters phrased it, "He doctored an unmarried girl who was in a family way. She lost the baby and died. They went after him pretty strong for that." Once more friends paid bail to free the priest; once more he filed a demurrer which delayed the trial.

Resumed in April, the trial caused a sensation. The girl's mother testified that she had taken her daughter home from Flaherty's house and that during the night she suffered much pain and said that she had been operated on. The mother called in two doctors, but the girl died the next day. Her story was substantiated by her son and another daughter. The two physicians claimed that death was due to septic poisoning following an abortion.

Acting both as counsel and witness for the defense, Father Flaherty swore he had been far away from the girl at the time he was alleged to have performed the operation. His brother, William, who then lived with him, said that the girl was not in the house on the dates in question. Claiming that her death was due to peritonitis, Flaherty asserted he was the best man in the county in his knowledge of obstetrics.

The jury convicted him of manslaughter in the first degree, and he was sentenced to from seven to fourteen years in prison. By then it should have surprised no one that he immediately obtained an order staying his sentence and, three weeks later, a certificate of reasonable doubt, releasing him from prison.

What did surprise everyone was the next act of this melodrama. Father Flaherty's housekeeper had disappeared the previous November. Now in May, 1926, her cruelly mutilated body was washed ashore on Lake Ontario. Submerged for five months, the body had a deep knife wound in the abdomen. Some said that this wound resulted from a surgical operation done by an experienced surgeon, though how this conclusion was reached was never explained. "Who had lately claimed to be the best obstetrician in the county?" people asked. "And isn't an obstetrician the next thing to a surgeon?"

Almost a year to the day after his arrest, the priest, now represented by two lawyers, was granted not only a stay of trial, but also an order requiring the district attorney to show cause why the trial should not be held in another county. There followed three months during which the Appelate Court sent the case back for a re-trial because of technical errors committed the first time. Finally in April the trial was held in Syracuse and resulted in a hung jury. A third trial was necessary.

This time the defense introduced witnesses who stated that

they had seen the pregnant girl leave Father Flaherty's house at the times he said she did. But the D.A. produced time sheets from these people's employers destroying their stories. It must have been a bright day in October, 1927, when the verdict against him was announced, for Father Flaherty remarked, "Just think of going to prison on such a perfect day! It is not pleasant for a man of my age to think of what the future means." His sentence was five to ten years in the State prison in Auburn, the town where he had gone to high school. His lawyers' motion for a new trial was denied, as was their application for a certificate of reasonable doubt.

"Personally he is a mightly likeable man and has dozens of friends who remain intensely loyal to him," wrote the *Livingston Republican* editor. "He is charitable, free-hearted, genial and friendly and a man of great force. But the courts of this county don't like him. He has been before them and kept them busy for years, and they are gratified now that he has been convicted and sentenced, not as individuals, but as officers of the law and the courts."

During his six years in prison, Father Flaherty worked on a book about prison reform. Its theme was that incarceration does not rehabilitate convicts and that society could prevent crime by removing its causes. When, after six years, he was released on parole, he returned to Mt. Morris to find that some of his supporters had refurbished his home. Afterward he told one friend that everyone should spend some time at the prison farm, that it was a good vacation. To another, he said, "When I went to prison I had good health, and now that I'm released I have better health." Still another acquaintance recalls his saying, "I'm going to write a book called '*Via Crucis, Via Christi*,' meaning 'The Way of the Cross, the Way of Christ.'"

For the next six years from 1933 to 1939, he carried on his ministry to others, but with less of his old flamboyance. Near the end of his life when asked how he felt, he answered, "*I* feel fine, but this old body of mine is wearing out." When he died of a heart attack in 1939 at the age of 83, his funeral was a Requiem Mass in St. Patrick's Church, Mt. Morris, conducted by the pastor, the Rev. William Rafferty. In contrast to the funeral, which was not publicly announced, the priest's burial in Baldwinsville, N. Y., his birthplace, was attended by several hundred people.

Was he saint or sinner? When the writer Carl Carmer asked Charles Flaherty to tell him his life story, he refused, saying that a man's career may best be judged by whatever of his work lives on after him. And how to assess that verdict? When one asks about him today in Mt. Morris and nearby towns, the memories are as contradictory as the man himself.

One woman recalls how as a little girl she was frightened of him with his large build, big black hat and tall cane, another that he always spoke cordially to her as a child. He had such a habit of brandishing that cane about when his temper flared that friends begged him to leave it at home. Yet this same man, called in to treat an elderly person's skin rash which defied physicians, tenderly bathed him every morning and brought about his recovery.

Some old-timers relish the story of how he irked a priest officiating at a burial. When he threw only one handful of dirt on the casket, Father Flaherty urged him to throw on more. Again he instructed, "Throw on a little more," to which the priest retorted, "You be quiet, or I'll throw you in there!" Once, seeing a local policeman roughly arrest a drunken woman, he admonished him to treat her with the respect due all women.

Many speak of his trudging along country roads, the very picture of St. Francis-like humility. But one person remembers his being chauffered in a long black limousine and sitting squarely in the middle of the back seat, "like the Pope." A fellow priest recalls Father Flaherty's neighbors had an almost superstitious fear that, if they harmed him in any way, they would suffer the consequences. His obituary in the *Livingston Republican* stated prudently, "While his career was varied, he was always the champion of the poor."

A revealing tribute appeared a week after his death in a letter to the local newspaper written by the president of the Frederick Douglass Mutual Aid Society. "Some years ago," it began, "members of my race started to complain of the unjust treatment they were forced to accept. My people on the whole are poor. They must accept the poorest compensation for their labors. . . .

"We found our way to the door of Father Flaherty, begging for knowledge, asking how we could help ourselves to be accepted as better citizens. We were not driven away. He invited us to sit down at his table and carefully explained the complicated workings of political machinery. He advised us to organize and to support the candidate who treated us justly. . . .

"To any who ridicule this old man, I say you didn't know what was inside the cup. Father Flaherty was a parent to all humanity, a helpmeet willing to share the bumps of the road with any brother in distress."

Making the point that it is impossible to judge Father Flaherty, one of his contemporaries has said, "You shouldn't ask, 'What do you know about Father Flaherty?' but only 'What do you *hear* about him?'" It is enough to say that this was as provocative and colorful a character as ever lived in Livingston County.

SOURCES

Carmer, Carl, *Listen for a Lonesome Drum*
Rochester Democrat and Chronicle, Nov. 16, 1939
Livingston Republican, Apr. 20, 1893 et passim
McNamara, Rev. Robert F., *The Diocese of Rochester, 1868-1968*
Residents of Mt. Morris and Geneseo, Personal interviews
The People Against Charles Flaherty

Kate Gleason, Builder

"She should have been a boy!" the neighbors exclaimed of Kate Gleason (1865–1933). The daughters of these respectable Rochesterians wore long curls and "sewed a fine seam." Kate did all she could to act like a boy, wearing her short hair straight and trying to keep up with her older brother, Tom, and his friends. "They didn't want me," she later recalled, "but I earned my right. If we were jumping from the barn roofs, I chose the highest spot; if we vaulted fences, I picked the tallest. It took just that added bit of daring to outdo the rest."

Little Kate adored Tom, who taught her to read before she was four. In return, she sat on a horseblock in front of their house and called out to any passing boy who was as large as Tom or larger, "You don't dare fight my brother!" When any responded to this challenge, Tom appeared and usually polished off the upstart. Later Kate's Irish-born parents, William and Ellen (McDermot) Gleason, sent her to Nazareth Convent parochial school where the sisters evidently failed to make a little lady of her.

When she was eleven, Tom died, which was a financial hardship for the family, since he had been his father's right-hand man in the small machine shop which Gleason operated. "Oh, if Kate had only been a boy," the beleaguered man remarked to his wife one day. Overhearing this, Kate was miserable to think that she had in any way failed her father and resolved to fill Tom's place.

The next Saturday she climbed onto a stool in the machine shop and demanded work. Smilingly, Gleason handed her some bills to make out, then at the end of the day realized how serious she was and paid her a dollar. Throughout her high school years, she studied from four until eight in the morning and worked as the shop's bookkeeper after school and on Saturdays. Watching the men work and asking questions, she learned much about mechanics. Again neighbors criticized the Gleasons, this time for stinginess. But her parents supported her determination. Her mother was a suffragist and friend of Susan B. Anthony, who encouraged the girl. "I owe a great deal of my inspiration to her," Miss Gleason said later. "She showed me that women could take an active part in outside affairs."

A few occupations had opened to women, though engineering was distinctly not one of them, when Kate entered Cornell University in 1884. Within the year, her father found that he could not afford to keep the bookkeeper who had replaced her, and she had to leave college. As Kate resumed her duties at the Gleason Works, she resolved to teach herself as much as her classmates were learning at Cornell. In every moment she could spare from her office work, she tried her hand at all the shop's operations.

In 1874 William Gleason had invented a machine to cut bevel gears, which are a pair of toothed wheels with non-parallel working surfaces that transmit mechanical power around angles. Bevel gears had previously been cut and filed by hand, a method both inexact and expensive, and his invention produced uniform assemblies with standardized parts. Kate had such a thorough understanding of the enginering theory behind the Gleason gear-cutter and of its possibilities that she often went to the plants of customers to solve problems involving them. Many a Rochester mechanic shook his head in disbelief that a young girl could do "a man's work" so expertly. In 1888 she returned to Cornell as a special student in the Sibley College of Engineering, the first of the women later nicknamed "Sibley Sues." Called home again, she attended night school classes at Mechanics Institute (later Rochester Institute of Technology).

When a lull in the economy reduced sales of their machines, Kate argued with her father that she should be allowed to go on the road to sell them. She particularly wanted to go after the large order of a certain company, and Gleason gave in to her entreaties. As a concession to convention, he had her say that she had come to the firm's city to attend an exhibition being held there. The plant official whom she saw happened to be new at his job and, as she said, was more scared of her than she of him. Sensing his timidity, she lost her own fears and obtained an order for $10,000-worth of tools.

At first Kate assumed that she would be at a disadvantage as the only traveling saleswoman in a business otherwise limited to men. But she found that, however much factory executives may have disapproved of her, they were curious to see her, giving her an advantage over her male competitors. From her own hard experience, Susan B. Anthony had taught her, "Any advertising is good. Get praise if possible, blame if you must, but never stop being talked about."

"In those days I was a freak," Miss Gleason said later. "I talked of gears when a woman was not supposed to know what a gear was." Yet she claimed that, thanks to her father's fine reputation, she experienced no hard knocks. One disadvantage which she could not overcome was the restriction of that time against a woman's taking a man to lunch. Once she knew that a certain foundry owner had been entertained by all her competitors, so thought her chances were poor. But as she reported, "I breezed in with a good yarn and got the order—on the sheer merit of the machine I was selling."

Kate's younger brothers, James and Andrew, had joined Gleason Works, concentrating on design and manufacture, when she became secretary-treasurer as well as chief sales person in 1890. As the plant prospered, the number of employees grew from the original twelve to 125. Then in the panic of 1893, sales became few and far between. Kate felt that the one ray of hope in the firm's prospects was its bevel gear planer, and she persuaded her father and brothers to shift production to it. "Gears wear out much quicker than tools," she said. "We could sell to the same people year after year. Nobody has such a machine as ours!"

The next year Kate traveled on a cattle boat to introduce the gear planer to industries in England, Scotland, France and Germany. She wore only one dress during the entire trip, but when Miss Anthony afterward advised her to pay more attention to her appearance, she decided to use clothes as a way to increase sales. She had her hair dressed becomingly, wore ultra-feminine dresses and carried a muff trimmed with violets. Twenty years later customers appreciatively remembered some of her outfits. "I learned to love clothes and to use clothes," she commented.

At first the Gleason gears and gear planer were sold primarily to bicycle manufacturers, but as the automobile industry emerged at the start of the new century, Kate foresaw a bright future for their products and developed added markets. Fanciful tales about her circulated throughout the industry. The story that she carried a tool bag and wore overalls brought her 200 letters proposing marriage. Once, having noticed that a Gleason gear planer in a customer's shop had a loud squeak, she found the cause and reported it to her father, who sent a man to adjust the machine. The shop owner endlessly told how "Old Man Gleason himself had never fixed that noise, and then his girl came along and fixed it in two minutes!"

Showing people about his plant, Henry Ford customarily pointed out the gear planer, saying, "There is the most remarkable work ever done by a woman. That machine is a marvel, and Kate Gleason invented it." Though he was set right many times, Henry Ford continued to tell the story his way. Possibly in the same wrong belief, the American Society of Mechanical Engineers was to elect Kate Gleason to membership in 1914.

The early auto makers soon dwindled down to a few giant companies which bought special parts from small suppliers. Gleason Works discontinued other items and came to dominate the gear-cutting machinery market as well as becoming a leading Rochester industry. When a larger plant was needed, Kate recalled a remark of her father's about European cathedrals: "What a chance for a traveling crane!" and sent for photos and plans of many cathedrals. The factory was modeled after the cathedral at Pisa and the office building after the Pan-American Building in Washington.

In 1913 Miss Gleason retired from the company and embarked on the first of her independent careers. A small machine-tool factory in East Rochester had failed and, as one of the first women bankruptcy receivers in New York State, she was appointed to manage its affairs. Whereas the firm's creditors had hoped that she might retrieve ten percent on their investment, she not only repaid a $140,000 debt but also made a profit of $1,000,000 in little more than a year. Then in 1917 she took the place of the president of the First National Bank of Rochester, who went to war, becoming the nation's first woman president of a national bank. During her three years in banking, she mended the fortunes of another defunct business. A builder of houses to whom the bank had loaned money had not been able to finish them; Kate took over the work and paid the loan.

This experience turned her efforts fom building up businesses to building homes, beginning with one in East Rochester for herself. Adapting its design from that of the Spanish palace, the Alhambra, she built it around a central patio, complete with mosaic fountains, palm trees and exotic flowers in rock gardens. Its glass roof worked on ball-bearings to open the court to the outdoors on pleasant days. A huge living room featured a Spanish-style fireplace with a brazier for burning charcoal, and her private suite on the second floor was reached by a wooden staircase which could be drawn up after her if she wished to be undisturbed.

As a banker, Gleason knew that East Rochester needed adequate low-cost housing. Besides, as she said, "Starting a new business in middle age, new problems, new conditions to cope with—it's splendid!" In 1919 she embarked on the construction of Concrest, 100 six-room concrete houses of standardized design. In every way she could devise, she applied to house construction the techniques of mass production that she had learned from automobile makers. For example, concrete was poured from a telescoping tower with a mixer, hopper and chute mounted on wheels for mobility. She borrowed from the Cadillac Company the device of providing each worker with a cabinet containing every item—and no more—that he needed for a job. She bought materials in great quantity, at the same time trying to eliminate waste even of such small items as nails. She wanted the fireproof houses to last "at least 100 years."

To make these inexpensive homes as attractive as possible, Kate had them placed in various positions on their sites in order to minimize their sameness. Of two stories plus a basement, they had six rooms with such features as built-in bookcases, kitchen cabinets, screens and window shades. In each kitchen she added a cookbook, mirror and powder puff. She made an area within the development a wooded park and planted many varied trees along its streets. A nine-hole golf course with a clubhouse was her gift to the new community. The houses cost $4,000 with a small down-payment and $40 per month mortgage.

At one time Kate had put up her Gleason Works stock as collateral and owed $600,000 on demand notes. She needed still more money to finish the houses, but local banks would lend her no more. A young woman whom she had earlier helped to start a business returned her kindness by persuading her own New York City bank to grant Kate a loan. In three years she had paid off all indebtedness. One more of her "firsts" came when the American Concrete Institute made her its first woman member.

"I want to go where people need me and work for them," Kate once said, and this wish led to her becoming the Lady Bountiful of a small village in France. Traveling there after World War I, she became concerned with the fate of Septmont, near Soissons, where 3,000 American soldiers had been killed and 7,000 wounded. She restored a twelfth-century castle tower as a home where she vacationed for three months every fall. She also converted a shop to a public library and built a movie theater as a memorial to the First Division of the American Expeditionary Force.

Returning to her work of providing mass-produced housing for low-income families, Gleason went to California to study adobe building in 1927. She drafted plans for similar houses of poured-concrete and bought several hundred lots in Sausalito outside San Francisco. Some homes were built there, but the project was aborted when the State of California took over the tract for public works facilities.

On the opposite coast, the Sea Island region near Beaufort, South Carolina, was also the site of her housing activities in the late 1920's. She planned to create a community of garden apartments on nearby Ladies' Island where artists, writers and other professional people of limited means could winter inexpensively. To give needed work to area residents, she tried to persuade a canning factory to open a branch there. These interests became linked with those in Septmont when she bought an island off the coast of Georgia as the place for a turkey farm. Knowing that French farmers excelled in raising turkeys, she planned to bring two French families there to teach their methods to Georgians. Meanwhile she took American-bred turkeys to France to improve the native stock. Unfortunately, Miss Gleason did not live to see these dreams realized, but it was the journey toward a goal, rather than its achievement, that fascinated her. "The greatest fun I have in life is building-up, trying to create," she once said.

In 1929 Miss Gleason began what she termed "unburdening herself" of her wealth in order to devote herself wholeheartedly to her Sea Island projects. Besides uncounted, and often anonymous, gifts to individuals, she arranged that her $1,400,000 estate would go to cancer research, a Rochester Public Library local history department, numerous local charities, Cornell University and, notably, Rochester Institute of Technology.

She had once told a magazine interviewer, "I wanted to demonstrate that a business woman can work as well as a man. My motto is 'I can if I will.'"

SOURCES

American Society of Mechanical Engineers, *Transactions*
Bennett, Helen C., "Kate Gleason's Adventures in a Man's Job"
Bird, Caroline, *Enterprising Women*
Chappell, Eve, "Kate Gleason's Careers"
Concrete Magazine, January, 1921
"Gleason, Kate," *Dictionary of American Biography Supplement 1*
The Gleason Works, 1865-1950
Kotel, Janet, "The Ms. Factor in A. S. M. E."
Lindley, Christopher, "Gleason, Kate"
Mechanical Engineering Magazine, July, 1973
New York Times, Jan. 10, 1933
Rochester Democrat and Chronicle, May 18, 1955; Jan. 10, 1933
Rochester Times Union, Jan. 9, 1933
Ross, Claire, "*Kate Gleason of Rochester, America's Pioneer Woman Merchant*"

Our Lady of the Genesee Abbey

Living in the Valley today is a group of men who as farmers and merchants are practical people. Yet most of their ways are not of this world or time. They are the monks of Our Lady of the Genesee Abbey, whose Trappist Order dates from a seventeenth-century reform of the Cistercian Order. Neither the pattern of their lives—prayer, study and work—nor their purpose has changed since then.

In 1949 Mr. and Mrs. Porter Chandler of Piffard, having read that the Trappist Abbey of Gethsemani in Kentucky was over-crowded, offered its abbot the gift of land to found a new community. It was a 570-acre farm in Piffard, which had belonged to Mr. Chandler's grandfather, Charles Wadsworth. After making several visits to look over the site and being invited by Bishop James Kearney to come to his diocese, Abbot James Fox decided to establish a monastery there and chose Father Gerard McGinley from Gethsemani as its prior.

With four other monks, Father McGinley went to Piffard in the spring of 1951 to renovate an old building on the farm. After spending several days with the Hubert Chanlers at Sweet Briar Farm in Geneseo, they stayed at Westerly, the Porter Chandlers' Piffard home. Roman Catholics of the area welcomed them enthusiastically, seeming to vie with one another, as Farther Gerard observed, in bringing gifts of food and helping with construction. Two women baked bread for the community to free the monks for building. Neighbors not of their faith viewed with interest this band of men in strange dress who rarely spoke, communicating in sign language only when necessary.

Having come from Kentucky, the monks were not prepared for the still-wintery April of the Valley, and the Chandlers' daughter, Judith, told Father Gerard that they must have warm clothes and heavy boots. In thanks for her concern, he wrote her a letter appointing her "the monastery's Lady Prioress, with the special duty of looking after the health of the monks."

In the confusion of moving out of Westerly when their quarters were ready, the monks took with them three garbage cans that belonged to the Chandlers. Mrs. Chandler asked to have them returned and was told, "Don't worry. Anything you give to the Lord's work will be returned to you one-hundred-fold."

To this she replied, "I don't want 300 garbage cans in heaven. I want three right here on earth!"

Nineteen members formed the community when Father Gerard planted a simple wooden cross on their highest point of land. On it was inscribed, "Foundation of the monastery of Blessed Mary of the Genesee, May 25, 1951. May God be glorified in all things. Serve the Lord with Gladness." One year later with a membership of thirty-three, the group was designated a "Domus Formata."

Until they built their chapel, the monks worshiped in nearby St. Raphael's Church with services open to the public, an unusual move for a cloistered order at that time. A parish member has recalled, "It was a beautiful experience to hear these virile, intelligent men chanting praises to heaven. They work as hard at making their songs of praise perfect as they do making their farm work successful."

Father Gerard has been described as a man with a fine sense of humor and appreciation of all of nature whose deep spirituality radiated from him. He had a remarkable ability to inspire others to share his conviction: "We cannot fail." His brother and sister-in-law came to help out for a month and stayed to devote their lives to the Order, he as contact person with the outside world, she as hostess of the guest house. Someone has said of Father Gerard that he asked for miracles and got them. He once wrote," We keep on building and buying materials even though we don't have a cent." Yet, for instance, just when piping was needed in a cowbarn, a contractor drove up with a load of pipe he could not use.

In their first years the community grew wheat, corn and barley, raised chickens and prize-winning Holstein cows as well as selling honey and cheese. The monk who baked for the group had been a cook in the Navy and used its recipe for bread, enriching it to his own taste. From the sale of a few extra loaves to visitors, this enterprise grew until stores for miles around were supplied with the popular Monks' bread, which became the monastery's chief source of income.

In the fall of 1954 the Trappists' Father Immediate came from France to visit the monastery, which by then had fifty members. Finding it self-sufficient and thriving, he ended its dependence on the mother house at Gethsemani, raising it from a monastery to an abbey. Thirty days later the monks unanimously elected Father Gerard abbot. The blessing of the new abbot by the bishop, which took place the next month, was the first ceremony of its kind ever held in the Rochester cathedral. The driver of the bus which took some of the monks to the service said it was a strange experience to drive thirty-five passengers who didn't talk.

In the next years the monks bought more land to insure their privacy, built a new barn and bakery and attracted more members. Dom Gerard left what he called "the valley of Mary's smile" in 1955 to attend the General Chapter of the Order in France and died there suddenly.

He was succeeded by Father Walter Helmstetter. After his retirement and a year's interim under the leadership of Father Regis Tompkins, the monks elected Father Jerome Burke abbot. Both Fathers Helmstetter and Burke lived as hermits after retiring. In 1972 the Rev. John Eudes Bamberger was elected abbot. Also a psychiatrist, Father Bamberger trained under the spiritual direction of the Trappist known to the world as Thomas Merton. In recent years he has invited the Rev. Henri Nouwen to live as a temporary member of the community. From this experience, Father Nouwen has written *The Genesee Diary*.

The abbey has gone through other changes since its early days. In 1974 and 1975 the monks built a new chapel of wood and stones which they collected and hauled from their land. Beautiful in its simplicity, it is graced by an Oriental-style garden and ringed by hilltop meadows. Visitors are now welcome at all services, and a number of laypersons attend them regularly. Basically, however, the ethos of the abbey is timeless. Attending a service there, one feels that the time-frame is not so much that of either the Middle Ages or the twentieth century as of eternity.

SOURCES

Our Lady of the Genesee Abbey
McGinley, Gerard, *A Trappist Writes Home*
Twomey, Gerald, Abbey of the Genesee Oral History Project

Samuel Bozzette, American Merchant

"What can I do for you today?" was the genial greeting of Samuel Bozzette (1881–1962) to the young couple who came to his Mt. Morris furniture store one day in the 1930's. To their reply that they were "just looking" he put them at their ease as he showed them around the shop, meanwhile sizing them up as dependable people who needed furniture but were short of funds. When he offered to let them buy what they wanted for small weekly payments, the pair selected a bedroom and a kitchen set. They wanted a radio as well, but decided that it would have to come later. The next day the husband telephoned Bozzette saying that there had been a mistake—the radio they had coveted had been delivered with the other furniture. "That wasn't a mistake," Bozzette answered. "I want you to keep it and enjoy it. Pay for it when you can."

An excellent salesman, Bozzette often trusted people, but was seldom fooled. He customarily arranged easy time payments for people who were temporarily "hard up." His saying "Pay what you can afford" sometimes meant as little as twenty-five cents a week. During the Depression of the thirties and when workers were ill or on strike, he let payments be postponed. Behind this policy lay memories of the hard times he had once endured.

Samuel Bozzette (whose name originally was Bozzetti) did not dwell on his childhood in Naples, Italy. As far back as he could recall, his father had wakened him and his brother in the mornings when it was still dark to go to a forest and cut trees. They worked all day with nothing to eat but chestnuts and black bread and, as he said, "Not enough of that." When Samuel was about fifteen, he and his brother came alone to Hoboken, New Jersey, where he found work driving teams of horses. Never having had a day's schooling in his life, this young man quickly learned to speak, read and write

201

English and joined some friends who moved to Mt. Morris in 1903. Having saved enough to buy a horse and wagon, he began selling rags and junk. At first he could not pay for these until after he had sold them, but it was not long before he was solvent. Sometimes he made extra profit by repairing and selling broken furniture.

In 1910 Samuel married the former Mary Manzie and bought a small house on the village's Main Street, converting its front section into a grocery store. While his wife tended the store and raised their three children, he traveled throughout the Valley selling fruit and vegetables from his wagon. Quick to see sales possibilities, he frequently bought an entire carload of an item at wholesale and managed to sell it at retail. The day came when he bought a truck to haul produce for a local canning factory, work which he supplemented by contracting to supply the labor of other truckers. He also rented land on the flats where he raised corn and asparagus and had an interest in a cider mill. The extent of his operations is shown in the line on a calendar he distributed: "Rags, rubber, iron, brass, copper, etc. Also groceries, dry goods, granite ware, hardware, notions."

Bozzette next switched his chief retail business from groceries to dry goods. Once, having located and sold a brass bed as a favor to a customer, he was struck by the difference in profit between marketing a pillow case and a bed, and he gradually changed his store over to home furnishings. As this business prospered, he expanded the building, which still housed his family behind the store. After his first wife's death, Bozzette married Mary DeGennaro of Buffalo, and they had four children. As the store's reputation grew, he had to expand the building and, despite the Depression, added parts to it every year during the 1930's.

Mrs. Bozzette had a flair for merchandising equal to her husband's as well as the ability to arrange furniture in the store for eye appeal. She became known among area furniture dealers as an astute business woman in her own right. The couple constantly plowed profits back into their business, denying themselves such frills as vacations. Their basic policy was to sell good quality at a medium price. "Always sell quality goods," Samuel would say, "otherwise, it gets to be a license to steal."

As has happened with each group of immigrants to this country, Italians in Mt. Morris in the early twentieth century were less than cordially received by those whose ancestors had arrived there on earlier voyages. But Bozzette was too much of an optimist to let this hinder his progress. He was busy applying his maxim, "Be honest, give good value and treat your customers right."

Bozzette had great patriotism for his adopted country where, as he said, "As long as you're willing to work, you can do anything you want to do." He was critical of Italian-Americans who would not learn English, and when Italy joined Germany in World War II, felt no sympathy for his homeland. "All I ever did there was starve," he said. As a member first of Assumption Church and later of St. Patrick's Church as well as of the Knights of Columbus, he contributed to charities and civic betterment, believing that he had a responsibility to share what the community had given him.

Bozzette's sons, Louis and Frank, joined him in the business in 1945 until Louis took it over in 1960, but the father was active in it until about four years before his death at age eighty-one. As he looked back, Samuel Bozzette had few regrets, though one was that he had never had the opportunity of an education. On the whole, he took pride in his accomplishments—not for having made money in itself, but for having taken care of his family and built up his store, making it a place where, as he would say, "things looked nice."

SOURCES

Bozzette family members, Personal and written interviews

Bibliography

Abell, Hattie. Unpublished reminiscence, University of Rochester, Department of Rare Books.

Abrams, George H. Letter to author.

Ackerman, Carl. *George Eastman*. Boston and New York: Houghton Mifflin Co., 1930.

Alsop, Gulielma F. *History of the Woman's Medical College, Philadelphia, Pennsylvania, 1850–1950*. Philadelphia: J.B. Lippincott Co., 1950.

"American Historical Trees," *Harper's New Monthly Magazine*, 24, No. 144 (May 1862).

American Society of Mechanical Engineers. Transactions, Vol. LVI, 1934.

Andrews, Edward D. "The New York Shakers and Their Industries," *New York State Museum Circular*, (Oct. 1930).

————. *The People Called Shakers*. New York: Oxford University Press, 1953.

Anthony, Katharine. *Susan B. Anthony*. Garden City, New York: Doubleday, 1954.

Armstrong, William H. *Warrior in Two Camps*. Syracuse: Syracuse University Press, 1978.

Balla, Wesley. Unpublished paper, "John Young of Geneseo, New York."

Barraco, Anthony M. "The Wadsworth Family of New York." Diss., University Microfilms: Ann Arbor, Michigan, May 1966.

Beale, Irene A. *William P. Letchworth: A Man for Others*. Geneseo, New York: Chestnut Hill Press, 1982.

Bennett, Helen C. "Kate Gleason's Adventures in a Man's Job," *American Magazine*, (Oct. 1928).

Bestor, Arthur E., Jr. "American Phalanxes, Vols. 1 and 2." Diss., University Microfilms: New Haven, Connecticut, 1970 (a xerox copy).

————. *Backwoods Utopias; The Sectarian and Owenite Phases of Communitarian Socialism in America, 1663–1829*. Philadelphia: University of Pennsylvania Press, 1950.

206

Biographical Review: The Leading Citizens of Livingston and Wyoming Counties, New York. Boston: Biographical Review Publishing Co., 1895.

Bird, Caroline. *Enterprising Women.* New York: W.W. Norton and Co., Inc., 1976.

Black, Sylvia R. "Seth Green, Father of Fish Culture," *Rochester History,* 6, No. 3 (1944), pp. 1–24.

Blinn, Henry C. *Diary of the Ministry's Journey to New Lebanon and Groveland.* Xerox of manuscript. East Canterbury, New Hampshire, 1856.

Boyd, William P. *History of the Town of Conesus, Livingston County, New York.* Conesus, New York: Boyd's Printing Establishment, 1887.

Boynton, Frances. *Temple Hill Academy.* Geneseo, N.Y., 1913. (Unpublished manuscript).

Bozette Family. Personal and written interviews.

Bragdon, Claude F. *More Lives Than One.* New York: A. A. Knopf, 1938.

Branch, Edward. *The Sentimental Years, 1830-1860.* New York: Hill and Wang, 1965.

Brodie, William. *Scrapbook, 1867-1875.* Milne Library, SUNY Geneseo, New York.

Brooks, Merle W. Personal interview.

Brunberg, G. David. *The Making of an Upstate Community.* Geneva, New York: Geneva Bicentennial Commission, 1976.

Bunnell, A.O., Ed. *Dansville, 1789-1902.* Dansville, New York: Instructor Publishing Co., 1902.

Carmer, Carl. *Listen for a Lonesome Drum.* New York: Sloane, 1950.

Carson, Gerald. "Bloomers and Bread Crumbs," *New York History,* 38, No. 3 (1957), pp. 294–308.

The Castilian. Sep. 12, 1902.

Chappell, Eve. "Kate Gleason's Careers," *Woman Citizen,* (Jan. 1926).

Colvin, Fred H. "Sixty Years With Men and Machines," *Journal of American Society of Mechanical Engineers.*

Concrete Magazine, (Jan. 1921).

Conklin, William D. "The Jackson Health Resort," Unpublished manuscript, 1971.

Costa, Erville. "Claude F. Bragdon, Architect, Stage Designer and Mystic," *Rochester History,* 29, No. 4 (Oct. 1967), pp. 1–20.

Cowan, Helen I. "Charles Williamson," *Rochester Historical Society. Publications, Fund Series,* 19 (1941), pp. 58–144.

Crapsey, Algernon. *The Last of the Heretics.* New York: A. A. Knopf, 1924.

————. "Lewis Henry Morgan," *Rochester Historical Society. Publications, Fund Series* 2 (1923), pp. 1–27.

Cross, Whitney R. *The Burned-over District: The Social and Intellectual History of Enthusiastic Religion in Western New York, 1800-1850.* Cornell University Press, 1950.

DeLong, Hermon W., Sr., Compiled by William D. Conklin. *Boyhood Reminiscences With Other Sketches.* Dansville, New York: W.D. Conklin, 1982.

Denison, Frances H. *Scrapbook.* Milne Library, SUNY Geneseo, New York.

Dewey, Charles A. "Sketch of the Life of Lewis Henry Morgan with Personal Reminiscences," *Rochester Historical Society. Publications, Fund Series,* 2 (1923), pp. 29–45.

Dictionary of American Biography. New York: C. Scribner's Sons, 1928–58; Numerous articles, see chapter sources.

Dockstader, Frederick J. *Great North American Indians.* New York: Van Nostrand Reinhold, 1977.

Doty, Lockwood L. *A History of Livingston County, New York.* Geneseo, New York: E. E. Doty, 1876.

Doty, Lockwood R. *History of Livingston County, New York.* Jackson, Michigan: W. J. VanDeusen, 1905.

Douglass, Frederick. *Life and Times Written by Himself.* Boston: DeWolf, Fiske, 1892.

Doyle, Sir Arthur Conan. *The History of Spiritualism.* New York: George H. Doran Co., 1926.

Ehrenreich, Barbara and Deirdre English. *Witches, Midwives and Nurses: A History of Women Healers.* Old Westbury: The Feminist Press, 1973.

Eisenberger, Bernard Weisberger. *They Gathered at the River.* Boston and Toronto: Little Brown, 1958.

Encyclopedia Americana, International Edition, 1982.

Fairchild, Herman L. "Henry Augustus Ward," *Rochester Academy of Science Proceedings,* 5 (1919).

Farrington, Frank. "He That Keeps Them Awake," *Hobbies,* (Oct. 1946).

Filler, Louis. "Frances Willard," In *McGraw Hill Encyclopedia of World Biography,* 1973.

Fillmore, Millard. *Millard Fillmore Papers, Vol. 1.* Ed. Frank Severance. Buffalo: Buffalo Historical Society, 1907.

Finney, Charles G. *Memoirs.* New York: A.S. Barnes & Co., 1876.

Fisher, Rosalind. *The Stone Strength of the Past.* Geneseo, New York: SUNY Geneseo, New York, 1971.

Fisher, Sidney. "A Philadelphia Perspective." In *Diary 1834-1871.*

Philadelphia: Historical Society of Pennsylvania, 1967.

Foster, Abram. "Eastman." In *McGraw Hill Encyclopedia of World Biography*. New York: McGraw Hill, 1973.

"George Eastman, 1854-1954," In *Genesee Country Scrapbook*. Rochester: Rochester Historical Society, 1954.

Glasgow, W. Melancthon. *History of the Reformed Presbyterian Church in America.* 1888.

Gilchrist, Donald. "Bibliography of Lewis Henry Morgan," *Rochester Historical Society. Publications, Fund Series*, 2 (1923), pp. 83-97.

The Gleason Works, 1865-1950. Rochester, New York: The Gleason Works, 1950.

Gordon, Elizabeth. *Story of the Life and Work of Cordelia Greene, M.D.* Castile: The Castilian, 1925.

Grayon, Benson. *The Unknown President: The Administration of Millard Fillmore*. Washington, D.C.: University Press of America, 1981.

Harmon, Isabel F. *The Early Families of Caledonia.* Unpublished manuscript, Caledonia, New York, 1946.

Harper, Ida H. *The Life and Work of Susan B. Anthony*. Indianapolis and Kansas City: The Bowen-Merrill Co., 1898-1908.

Hatch, Alden. *The Wadsworths of the Genesee*. New York: Coward-McCann, Inc., 1959.

Hayes, Catherine D., Ed. *The University of Rochester Library Bulletin*, 26, No. 3 (1971), pp. 53-162.

Hennington, C.W. "Dr. Edwin G. Munn," *Buffalo Medical Journal*, 68, No. 5 (Dec. 1912).

History of Allegany County, New York. New York: F.W. Beers & Co., 1879.

Holloway, Mark. *Heavens on Earth*. New York: Dover Publications, 1966.

Holmes, William H. "Biographical Memoir of Lewis Henry Margan," *Rochester Historical Society. Publications, Fund Series*, 2 (1923), pp. 61-76.

Holtzman, S.F. "Louis Henry Morgan," In *McGraw Hill Encyclopedia of World Biography*. New York: McGraw-Hill, 1973.

Hosmer, William H.C. *Later Lays and Lyrics*. Rochester, New York: D.M. Dewey, 1873.

———. *The Poetical Works of William H.C. Hosmer*. New York: Redfield, 1854.

Hubbard, J. Niles. *An Account of Sa-go-ye-wat-ha, or Red Jacket and His People, 1750-1830*. Albany: J. Munsell's Sons, 1886.

———. *Sketches of Border Adventures in the Life and Times of Major Moses VanCampen*. Fllmore, New York: Jno. S. Minard, 1893.

Jenkins, John S. *Lives of the Governors of the State of New York.* Auburn, New York: Derby & Miller, 1851.

Jenson, David. "A Business Started With a Pebble," *Lapidary Journal,* 6, No. 5 (Dec. 1952).

Johnson, Paul E. *A Shopkeeper's Millennium: Society and Revivals in Rochester New York, 1815-1837.* New York: Hill and Wang, 1978.

Kamer, Fran. "The Shakers at Sonyea," *The New York-Pennsylvania Collector,* VI, No. 6 (Aug. 1981).

Katz, Herbert and Marjorie. *Museums, U.S.A.* Garden City, New York: Doubleday and Co., 1965.

Kenway, Mary M. "Portraits of Red Jacket," *Antiques Magazine,* 54, No. 2 (Aug. 1948), pp. 100-101.

Kolecki, John. "Red Jacket, the Last of the Senecas." Diss. Niagara University, 1976.

Kotel, Janet. "The Ms. Factor in A.S.M.E.," *Mechanical Engineering Magazine,* (July 1973).

Letchworth, William P. "Dancing Sal," Unpublished papers, Milne Library, SUNY Geneseo, New York.

Lindley, Christopher. "Gleason, Kate," In *Notable American Women, 1607-1950.* Volume 2 (1971), pp. 51-52.

Livingston County Historical Society Annual Reports. 1879, 1883, 1885, 1904, 1918.

Livingston Republican, Numerous articles, see chapter sources.

Lutz, Alma. *Susan B. Anthony.* Boston: Beacon Press, 1959.

Marion, John F. *Philadelphia Medica.* n.p.: Smith Kline Corp., 1975.

McGinley, Gerard. *A Trappist Writes Home.* Milwaukee: Bruce Publishing Co., 1960.

McIlvaine, Rev. J.H. "Life and Works of Lewis Henry Morgan," *Rochester Historical Society. Publications, Fund Series,* 2 (1923), pp. 47-60.

McKelvey, Blake. *Rochester, The Flower City, 1855-1890.* Cambridge, Mass: Harvard University Press, 1949.

————. *Rochester, The Quest for Quality, 1890-1925.* Cambridge, Mass.: Harvard University Press, 1956.

————. *Rochester, The Water-Power City, 1812-1854.* Cambridge, Mass.: Harvard University Press, 1945.

McLoughlin, William G., Jr. *Modern Revivals.* New York: The Ronald Press Co., 1959.

McNall, Neil A. "The First Half-Century of Wadsworth Tenancy," *Cornell Studies in American History, Literature and Folklore,* 2 (1945).

————. "The Landed Gentry of the Genesee," *New York History,* 26

(1945), pp. 162–176.

McNamara, Rev. Robert F. *The Diocese of Rochester 1868–1968*. Rochester, New York: Diocese of Rochester, 1968.

Melcher, Marguerite. *The Shaker Adventure*. Princeton University Press, 1941.

Minard, John S. *The Story of John Barker Church*. Belmont, 1916.

Morantz, Regina. "The Lady and Her Physician," In *Clio's Consciousness Raised*. Ed. Mary Hartman and Lois Banner. New York: Harper and Row, 1974.

Neblette, C.B. "George Eastman," In *Encyclopedia Americana*, International Edition, 1982.

Numbers, Ronald L. "Dr. Jackson's Water Cure and Its Influence on Adventist Health Reform," *The Adventist Heritage*, 1, No. 1 (Jan. 1974).

"Obituary of Edwin Munn," *Rochester Democrat and Chronicle*, December 23, 1847.

"Obituary of Kate Gleason," *New York Times*, January 10, 1933.

Our Lady of the Genesee Abbey. Rochester: Christopher Press, 1953.

Parker, Arthur C. "Charles Williamson, Builder of the Genesee Country," *Rochester Historical Society. Publications, Fund Series*, 6 (1927), pp. 1–34.

_____. *Red Jacket, Last of the Seneca*. New York: McGraw Hill, 1952.

Parker, Jane M. *Rochester: A Story Historical*. Rochester, New York: Scrantom, Wetmore and Co., 1884.

Parker, Kathleen. "The Wadsworths' Political and Public Service Contributions to the United States," Unpublished manuscript, Milne Library, SUNY Geneseo, New York.

Parsons, Rev. Levi and Samuel L. Rockfellow, Eds. *Centennial Celebration, Mt. Morris, New York*. Mt. Morris, New York: J.C. Dickey, 1894.

Patchett, Anna. *Historically Speaking*. Geneseo, New York: Livingston County Historical Society, 1978.

Pearson, Henry Greenleaf. *James S. Wadsworth of Geneseo*. New York: Charles Scribner's Sons, 1913.

Peck, William F. "Elisha Johnson, President of the Village and Mayor of Rochester," *Rochester Historical Society. Publications, Fund Series*, 6 (1927), pp. 291–296.

Peer, Sherman. "The Genesee River Country: Historical Sketches," Unpublished manuscript, Milne Library, SUNY Geneseo, 1954.

The People Against Charles Flaherty. Privately printed pamphlet.

Phelan, Helene C. *Allegany's Uncommon Folk*. Almond, New York: Helene C. Phelan, 1978.

Quarles, Benjamin, Comp. *Frederick Douglass*. Englewood Cliffs, New

Jersey: Prentice-Hall, 1968.

Renwick, James. "Life of James Wadsworth," *Monthly Journal of Agriculture*, 2, No. 4 (Oct. 1846), pp. 145–156.

Rochester Democrat and Chronicle, January 10, 1933 and May 18, 1955.

Rochester Times Union, January 9, 1933.

Rollick, Jeffrey. "Genesee Valley Memories," Recorded Oct. 3, 1976.

Root, Mary. *History of the Town of York, Livingston County, New York*. Caledonia, New York: Big Springs Historical Society, 1940.

Rorabaugh, W.J. *The Alcoholic Republic: An American Tradition*. New York: Oxford University Press, 1979.

Ross, Claire. "Kate Gleason of Rochester, America's Pioneer Woman Merchant," *Pictorial Review*.

Samson, W.A. *The Treaty of the Big Tree*. Bunnell and Oberdorf Press, 1895.

Scherer, John L. "The Dissolution of a Shaker Community," *The New York-Pennsylvania Collector*, VI (Oct. 1981).

Seaver, James. *A Narrative of the Life of Mary Jemison*. New York: American Scenic and Historic Preservation Society, 1963.

Seth Green and the Caledonia Fish Hatchery. Caledonia, New York: Big Springs Historical Society, 1964.

Sheer, Hazel M. *Tales From Allegany County*. Wellsville: Hazel Sheer, 1962.

Shryock, Richard H. *Medicine in America: Historical Essays*. Baltimore: The Johns Hopkins Press, 1966.

Sigourney, L.H. *Scenes in My Native Land*. Boston: James Monroe and Co., 1845.

Sklar, Kathryn Kish. "All Hail to Pure Cold Water!," *American Heritage*, 26, No. 1 (1974), pp. 64–69, 100–101.

———. *Catharine Beecher: A Study in American Domesticity*. New Haven and London: Yale University Press, 1973.

Slater, John R. "Lewis Henry Morgan," In *Genesee Country Scrapbook, Volume VI*. Rochester, New York: Rochester Historical Society, 1955.

Smith, James H. *History of Livingston County, New York*.Syracuse, New York: D. Mason & Co., 1881.

Sterling, Philip and Rayford Logan. *Four Took Freedom*. Garden City, New York: Doubleday, 1967.

Stone, William L. *The Life and Times of Sa-Go-Ye-Wat-Ha or Red Jacket*. Albany: Munsell, 1866.

Strong, Augustus H. "Henry A. Ward: Reminiscence and Apreciation," *Rochester Historical Society. Publictions, Fund Series*, 1 (1922), p. 256.

Strong, George Templeton. *Diary, Volume 2*. Eds. Allan Nevins and

Milton H. Thomas. New York: The Macmillan Co., 1952.

Swanton, Carolyn. "Dr. Algernon S. Crapsey: Religious Reformer," *Rochester History*, 42, No. 1 (Jan. 1980).

Taussig, Ellen. "Greene Sanatorium," *Buffalo Evening News Magazine*, February 23, 1952.

"Temple Hill, Geneseo," In *A Day in the Historic Genesee Valley*. Society for the Presevation of Landmarks in Western New York, Rochester, New York, 1952.

Thornton, Winifred K. "A History of the Church Mansion, Belvidere," *New York History*, 31, No. 3 (1950), pp. 294–307.

Tomlinson, George B. *From Youth to Seventy*. LeRoy, New York: Le Roy Times Co., 1894.

Truax, Rhoda. *The Doctors Warren of Boston, First Family of Surgery*. Boston: Houghton Mifflin Co., 1968.

Turner, Orsamus. *History of the Pioneer Settlement of Phelps and Gorham's Purchase*. Rochester: William Alling, 1851.

_____. *Pioneer History of the Holland Purchase of Western New York*. Buffalo: Jewett, Thomas and Co., 1850.

Twomey, Gerald. "Abbey of the Genesee Oral History Project," Milne Library, SUNY Geneseo, Recorded, 1975.

The University of Rochester: The first One Hundred Years. Rochester: University of Rochester Centennial Committee, 1950.

Vietor, Agnes, Ed. *A Woman's Quest: The Life of Marie A. Zakrzewska, M.D.* New York and London: D. Appleton and Co., 1972.

Wadsworth, Elizabeth. Letter to Mrs. Sigourney, 1843.

Walker, Peter F. *Moral Choices: Memory, Desire and Imagination in 19th-Century American Abolitionism*. Baton Rouge, Louisiana: State University Press, c.1978.

Walsh, Mary R. *Doctors Wanted: No Women Need Apply*. New Haven and London: Yale University Press, 1977.

Ward, Roswell. "Henry A. Ward: Museum Builder to America," *Rochester Historical Society. Publictions, Fund Series*, 24 (1948).

Washington, Booker T. *Frederick Douglass*. Jacobs, c.1906.

Willard, Frances E. *Glimpses of Fifty Years, The Autobiography of an American Woman*. Boston, Mass.: G.M. Smith & Co., 1889.

Winkelman, John H. "The Wadsworth Library (1869–1955) in the Genesee Valley," *Journal of Library and Information Science*, No. 2 (Oct. 1979).

Wood, Ann Douglas. In *Clio's Consciousness Raised*. Eds. Mary Hartman and Lois Banner. New York: Harper and Row, 1974.

Zakrzewska, Marie A. "Fifty Years Ago—A Retrospect," *The Woman's Medical Journal*, 1, No. 10 (1893), pp. 193–195.

Index

216

220

224

Wharton, Mary Craig 39
Wheeler, Charles 159
Whipple, Katherine (Mrs. George)
  179,180
White, Ellen G. 89
White House, The 59
White Woman of the Genesee 113
Whitmore, Sarah 45
Whittier, John Greenleaf 130,162
Wilkes-Barre Fort 22
Wilkes-Barre (Pa.) Gazette 16
Willard, Frances E. 139,151,152,153
Williamsburg, N.Y. 10,13,14,18,46,54
Williams College 66,141
Williamson, Charles 7,10,13,14,15,16,
  17,18,54,58
Wisconsin 8,151
Wiscoy, N.Y. 162
Wolcott, Naomi 34
Wolf Clan 113
Woman's Christian Temperance
  Union 153,154

Wood, Ann 172
Wood, Ann Jackson 135
Wood, Gen. James 172
Wood, Judge Walter 79
Woodruff, Bushrod W. 157,158
Woodruff, Mrs. ____ 158
World War I 176,194
Wright, Elder ____ 156
Wright, Henry Gardner 134
Wyoming County 66
Wyoming County Med Assoc. 136
Wyoming, Pa. 63

Yale University 33,39,50,51
Yonnondio 8
York, Village of 76,82,91,92
Young, John 81,82,83,119,172,175
Yates Academy 123

Zakrzewska, Dr. Marie 130,131,135,
  139

Index Compiled and writted by Francis Hoy, Historian,
Town of Orangeville, Wyoming County, N.Y.